READING THE BIBLE
WITH
HEART AND MIND

READING THE BIBLE
WITH
HEART & MIND

TREMPER LONGMAN III

NAVPRESS®
BRINGING TRUTH TO LIFE

OUR GUARANTEE TO YOU

We believe so strongly in the message of our books that we are making this quality guarantee to you. If for any reason you are disappointed with the content of this book, return the title page to us with your name and address and we will refund to you the list price of the book. To help us serve you better, please briefly describe why you were disappointed. Mail your refund request to: NavPress, P.O. Box 35002, Colorado Springs, CO 80935.

The Navigators is an international Christian organization. Our mission is to reach, disciple, and equip people to know Christ and to make Him known through successive generations. We envision multitudes of diverse people in the United States and every other nation who have a passionate love for Christ, live a lifestyle of sharing Christ's love, and multiply spiritual laborers among those without Christ.

NavPress is the publishing ministry of The Navigators. NavPress publications help believers learn biblical truth and apply what they learn to their lives and ministries. Our mission is to stimulate spiritual formation among our readers.

Library of Congress Catalog Card Number: 96-27858

ISBN 08910-99840

Some of the anecdotal illustrations in this book are true to life and are included with the permission of the persons involved. All other illustrations are composites of real situations, and any resemblance to people living or dead is coincidental.

Unless otherwise identified, all Scripture quotations in this publication are taken from the *HOLY BIBLE: NEW INTERNATIONAL VERSION* ® (NIV®). Copyright © 1973, 1978, 1984 by International Bible Society. Used by permission of Zondervan Publishing House. All rights reserved. Another version used is the *King James Version* (KJV).

Longman, Tremper.
     Reading the Bible with heart and mind / Tremper Longman, III.
          p. cm.
     ISBN 0-89109-984-0
     1. Bible—Hermeneutics. 2. Bible—Reading. 3. Bible—Criticism, interpretation, etc.
4. Bible—Use. 5. Spiritual life—Religious aspects—Christianity.
     BS476.L645 1997
     220.6'01—DC20

Printed in the United States of America

5 6 7 8 9 10 11 12 13 14 15 / 09 08 07 06 05 04

To Alice

CONTENTS

ACKNOWLEDGMENTS

The opportunity to write this book was a dream come true. Though I didn't let my publisher know this until contract negotiations were finished, I likely would have written it for nothing. The book's purpose is at the core of my passion: to reflect on God's Word and teach how to read it correctly—not just for intellectual knowledge, but for spiritual transformation. As I actually started to write, I realized my inadequacy for the task. I thank God that I had many competent and spiritually mature people to give me support and advice.

First, I would like to thank Steve Webb and Kathy Yanni for issuing the invitation to write. Kathy had just finished working with Dan Allender and me on *Cry of the Soul*, and I knew that any book she recommended I work on would be a worthwhile project. Second, I would like to thank David Hazard and Gary Wilde, both of whom served as editors on this project. They have each had a great influence on this book and have carefully shepherded my writing through the entire process. The final product is infinitely better than it would have been without their invaluable help. I deeply appreciate their rich insight and friendship.

Third, though his influence on this book has been indirect, I want to thank my longtime friend and writing companion, Dan Allender. Even though we didn't write this book together as we have a number of others, I've learned much through him and from him, not only about spiritual matters that affect daily life but about how to read the Bible.

Last, but certainly not least, I express thanks and love to my wife, Alice, to whom this book is dedicated. Not only is she the love of my life, she's an example of godliness and spiritual devotion toward which I aspire.

Tremper Longman III

PREFACE

As I began this book, I thought often of Carmen. She had heard the gospel at a Christian rally in her dorm, and the message made a lot of sense to her. She was lonely; the Christians were neat people.

She started attending a Bible study that met for an hour, three nights a week, and she eventually trusted Christ as her Savior. She began reading her Bible every day. She liked the "love of God" parts but gradually found that she wasn't particularly inspired by the "old-fashioned stuff" about sin. And then, her roommates started to get on her case about spending so much time with those "religious nuts." So after a few months, she found excuses not to go to her study group. The excitement just wore off, and the Bible reading times became fewer and fewer. Something about it all began to go dry. Her Bible started gathering dust on her shelf.

SPIRITUAL IGNITION NEEDED

It's not uncommon; the excitement can wear off. And it doesn't just happen to the occasional new believer. I've found it in the most mature

Christians—those periods of time when the Bible seems to hold little attraction. Indeed, it's been a part of my own experience. Yet I take comfort in knowing that the most exemplary Christians of old, as well, attest to hitting such dry spells with the Word of God. Listen to John Bunyan, for example:

> I have sometimes seen more in a line of the Bible than I could well tell how to stand under, and yet at another time the whole Bible hath been to me as dry as a stick.[1]

This book seeks to ignite that dry stick, for the Scriptures are like fire; they enkindle the character of Christ within us if we will just stay close to them and let them do their heartwarming work. Once we experience that kind of igniting of our souls, we won't be able to stay away for long.

How about you? If you're interested in a renewed love for His Word, read on! I've organized the chapters under four parts:

Part I: The Bible's Transforming Power. Someone once said: "Other books were given for our *in*formation, the Bible was given for our *trans*formation." We begin by speaking of the Bible's transforming power through two analogies: the Bible is the seed that grows the character of Christ within us; it is also a mirror that reflects what is already there, what *needs* to be transformed. Both of these images, of course, tell of a genuine encounter with God.

Part II: The Receptive Heart. Truly, the Bible as the Word of God has an inherent power, but it is not a coercive power. That is, the Bible does not work its effects mechanically. We don't change just because we read it. Our minds may be engaged in the text, but something must happen in our hearts as well. In the parable of the sower (Matthew 13:18-23), the seed does not miraculously and independently transform itself into a flowering plant. The condition of the soil affects how well the seed takes root. Our hearts must be receptive to God's Word in the same way that soil must be rich and conducive to the development of deep roots and luxuriant growth. As Oliver Wendell Holmes once said: "What you bring away from the Bible depends to some extent on what you carry to it."

In this part of the book we begin with a discussion of lenses. What do lenses have to do with a receptive heart? Though it may not be apparent at first, this image does speak of our receptivity to God's Word, for we bring a *perspective* to the Bible every time we open its pages. If our perspective is thoroughly skewed or grossly smudged, then what enters our vision—what we "see" and understand with our minds—can hardly pierce into our hearts. So the two metaphors work well together.

Part III: The Understanding Mind. What are the perspectives— the attitudes, concerns, and passions—that characterize a receptive heart? In the first place, a receptive reader focuses on the object of the Word, Jesus Christ Himself. Further, he or she must approach the Bible with trust, for a trust in the Bible is at heart a trust in God Himself. Thus, in Part III, we raise the question of the Bible's integrity and explore how we can set our minds at ease about its authority and genuineness. We must be convinced that it truly is the Word of God in order to develop our deep passion for its transforming power within us.

Our passion for God Himself directly relates to our desire to know His Word and understand it aright. Just as we want to spend time and talk with a close friend, so we yearn to hear the voice of the One who knows us so well and speaks so directly to our hearts. We want to grow in our experience of listening to God's Word. And the better we understand the nature of His Word, the more clearly and accurately we will hear God. Therefore, we turn to an exploration of the seven crucial principles for interpreting the Bible.

Part IV: The Literary Cornucopia. Finally, I dedicate the bulk of the book to a survey of the marvelous variety of literary genres that make up the Bible. Like a horn of plenty overflowing with ripe vegetables, the Bible abounds with the fruits of history, law, poetry, prophecy, and other literary forms. We must understand the characteristics of each genre to know how the writers are speaking to us. An apple is not a tomato. An orange tastes different from a pear.

It is truly wonderful to realize that our God, the Creative Genius of the cosmos, has given us such variety and richness in His Word. He has let the personality of the writers flow through. Rather than handing down an antiseptic "Manual of Religious Instruction," He has allowed intensely personal artistry and music to flourish for our satisfaction. As you dig into this flourishing literary bounty, may God grant you an answer to the kind of prayer that covets a flowering of your inner being:

God stir the soil,
Run the ploughshare deep,
Cut the furrows round and round,

Overturn the hard, dry ground,
Spare not strength nor toil,
Even though I weep.
In the loose, fresh mangled earth
Sow new seed.
Free of withered vine and weed
Bring fair flowers to birth.[2]

WITH HEART AND MIND

The title of this book makes it clear that we need a whole-person engagement with the Word of God. When both heart and mind are in full swing, interacting with the Word is an awesome experience because it is a personal encounter with the living God.

My prayer for you as you begin this adventure is that you will not be merely informed but transformed. That is what happens when the Scriptures engage both heart and mind. And what better way to spend the best moments of our days than in fruitful involvement with the Scriptures?

In response to that question, I leave you with John Calvin's eloquent, one-sentence endorsement of Bible reading:

> Read Demosthenes or Cicero; read Plato, Aristotle, or any others of that class; I grant you that you will be attracted, delighted, moved, enraptured by them in a surprising manner; but if, after reading them, you turn to the perusal of the sacred volume, whether you are willing or unwilling, it will affect you so powerfully, it will so penetrate your heart, and impress itself so strangely on your mind that, compared with its energetic influence, the beauties of rhetoricians and philosophers will almost entirely disappear; so that it is easy to perceive something divine in the sacred Scriptures, which far surpasses the highest attainments and ornaments of human industry.[3]

PART I

THE BIBLE'S TRANSFORMING POWER

1
THE WORD
IS THE SEED

The young man first encountered the warmth of God's Word on his mother's lap. Unfortunately, at the same time he felt his father's cold indifference to spiritual things. They were a middle-class family, his mother a devoted Christian. Yet his father had little time for "otherworldly nonsense." Thus began a subtle warfare for the boy's soul. His mother often spoke to him from the Scriptures while his father envisioned his son's business achievement and financial success.

The young man, headstrong and extremely bright, chose his own path. With a gang of friends, he terrorized the town. Once they vandalized a neighbor's pear orchard, stealing crates of harvested fruit and dumping them at a local hog farm "just for fun." His mother reminded him of the commandment "You shall not steal" with little effect.

Amazingly, the young man grew up to become a renowned philosopher, teaching at top academies where the wealthy and influential sent their children. But his wild streak ran deeper than ever. Different nights brought different women to his bed. Alcohol flowed. On weekends he partied at ocean-front resorts. Ironically, he took up a philosophy that directly challenged the things he had learned at his mother's feet, and for many years he worked to undermine her faith. When she told him to turn to the true God or be lost, her words fell on a stony heart.

What did this young man need? What would it take to change his life?

THE WORD: A TRANSFORMING POWER

Those are questions we could ask of anyone, including ourselves, for we all seek change and a more satisfying way of living. The premise of this book is that the Word of God is the single most powerful agent for transforming a life—whether the life of a young man living centuries ago or the life of a twentieth-century person like you or me. Reading and studying the Bible will transform each of us into someone truly beautiful—for the Bible ignites the character of Christ within us.

Jesus Himself proclaimed the Bible's transforming power in a story about farming (see Mark 4:1-20). Let's go back to the original scene and hear Him speak the words anew. He stands on the northern shore of the Sea of Galilee and the crowds press so close that He gets into a boat and launches out a bit from the shore. The people gather there at the banks of the sea and listen intently to every word.

Who were these folks, and why were they there? What were the young mother, the elderly grandfather, and the energetic teenager hoping to hear? Would you have been there, wanting to hear words ringing with heavenly truth and practical wisdom?

At any rate, as He did so often, Jesus spoke in a parable, drawing from everyday experience: a man flung seeds out onto the ground. In those days of hand seeding, farmers would scatter the seeds in a wide ark on their small plots of land. Since the Galilean soil was fertile but extremely rocky, the seeds met different fates as they landed on different parts of the field:

"Some fell along the path, and the birds came and ate it up. Some fell on rocky places, where it did not have much soil. It sprang up quickly because the soil was shallow. But when the sun came up, the plants were scorched, and they

withered because they had no root. Other seed fell among
thorns, which grew up and choked the plants, so that they
did not bear grain. Still other seed fell on good soil. It
came up, grew, and produced a crop, multiplying thirty,
sixty, or even a hundred times. (Mark 4:4-8)

Thus Jesus ended His story for the crowd on the shore, and they
were left to contemplate what it meant. However, when He returned
to the smaller circle of His disciples, Jesus interpreted His speech for
them. The seed is "the word," and the different fates of the seed tell
of the different ways people receive it.

"Some people are like seed along the path where the word
is sown. As soon as they hear it, Satan comes and takes away
the word that was sown in them. Others, like seed sown on
rocky places, hear the word and at once receive it with joy.
But since they have no root, they last only a short time.
When trouble or persecution comes because of the word,
they quickly fall away. Still others, like seed sown among
thorns, hear the word, but the worries of this life, the
deceitfulness of wealth, and the desires for other things,
come in and choke the word, making it unfruitful. Others,
like seed sown on good soil, hear the word, accept it, and
produce a crop—thirty, sixty or even a hundred times what
was sown." (Mark 4:14-20)

Most important for us is Mark 4:14, "The farmer sows the word."
Here Jesus identifies the seed with the word of the gospel, teaching
that the Word of God is a living seed that germinates in our souls and
sends its roots down deep, transforming our whole being. Notice
two important qualities of the Word:

First, like a seed, the Word is the agent of life. Some think of the
Bible only as a book that prepares us for death. Yet the Bible is the
place where we meet and develop a relationship with Jesus, who
offers "abundant life." Without Christ, life may have its short-term
enjoyments and successes, but deep down we know that there is as
much pain in life as there is joy. And, in any case, death brings it all
to an end.

With Christ, according to the Bible, we find ultimate meaning
and satisfaction. The joys and successes that we experience in this life
are glimpses of heaven in the present. Christians will suffer, sometimes

more intensely than those who do not believe. But Christians can have a rich peace in the midst of suffering because they know their pain is not arbitrary. And they have an even greater hope as they look to a future existence in the eternal bliss of God's presence.

Second, the seed of the Word is a catalyst for growth. The Word is the place we go if we want to mature, to reach our fullest potential in all areas of our lives. If we earnestly read the Bible with an openness to its divine author, it will change our minds, enrich our spirits, and guide us through each day. Nothing else is so powerful for change or so deeply fulfilling.

THE SEED: A LIVING POTENTIAL

How did the Word affect our young philosopher? Late one summer day, he was sitting on a bench in the garden of a wealthy friend. The sunlight on his back couldn't penetrate the cold deadness within. For months he'd felt empty. Sometimes his only feeling was the pain of this realization: his superior reasoning skills had never led him to lasting happiness. He recalled the words of Christ that his mother had spoken and sensed the beautiful light of God that wanted to flood his inner man. Yet he also remembered the lust that had constantly consumed him, how powerless he had been to oppose it. And the long, dark shadow of his own pride rose up to shield his soul from the guilt that struck at him like a piercing blade.

He did begin to see, though, how little he actually believed the self-centered philosophies he had taught. And he saw the faces of young students he'd led away from the pursuit of truth. He recalled the many young women he'd used and forgotten, under the guise of "love." He had thought that he was free. Now he saw what a prisoner to his own lusts he had always been.[1]

> I probed the hidden depths of my soul and wrung its pitiful secrets from it, and when I mustered them all before the eyes of my heart, a great storm broke within me. Somehow I flung myself down beneath a fig tree and gave way to the tears which now streamed from my eyes. For I felt that I was still the captive of my sins, and in misery I kept crying, "How long shall I go on saying, 'Tomorrow, tomorrow'? Why not now? Why not make an end of my ugly sins at this moment?"

He wanted to surrender, but years of stubborn independence and pride held him back. His heart longed for a new life and true freedom of spirit, but his struggle increased. And then the beckoning call of God came to him in the most mundane—and marvelous—way:

> I was asking myself these questions, weeping all the while with the most bitter sorrow in my heart, when all at once I heard the singing of a child in a nearby house. Whether it was the voice of a boy or girl I cannot say, but again and again it repeated the refrain, "Take it and read, take it and read." At this I looked up, thinking hard whether there was any kind of game in which children used to chant words like these, but I could not remember ever hearing them before.
>
> I stemmed my flood of tears and stood up, telling myself that this could only be a divine command to open my book of Scripture and read . . ."

Turning to the open Scriptures that rested on the bench beside him, his eyes fell on Romans 13:14: "Clothe yourselves with the Lord Jesus Christ, and do not think about how to gratify the desires of the sinful nature."

> In an instant, as I came to the end of the sentence, it was as though the light of confidence flooded into my heart and the darkness of doubt was dispelled . . . You, (God), converted me to yourself, so that I no longer placed any hope in this world but stood firmly upon the rule of faith.

The Word—like a living seed that had lain dormant inside for many years—burst into life in his soul. He fell on his face and surrendered to Christ. His life was changed. And the church was changed, and Western history, too. The man was Augustine, who eventually became the great bishop of the African church in Hippo. From his time (A.D. 354–430) until today, few have influenced the course of nations and cultures, and the lives of millions of believers, as he did—once the living Word of God harnessed his enormous intellect and passion to the service of Christ.

Yet such stories of transformation through the Word do not come only from the past. We find them everywhere today, too. I think of a prominent Palestinian Christian whom I know. When he was a young child, he witnessed the murder of his father at the hands of Israeli soldiers. Before his eyes, they dragged his father out into his backyard and shot him in the head. This young son grew up with the memory of his father's blood seeping into the sand where playmates had left their toys that same morning. He fed his cauldron of hurt, and he let it seethe, until it boiled into an intense hatred for all Israelis.

Then the boy met Christ. And as he got to know his Lord more intimately through the Scriptures, he found his whole personality being transformed. The physical body that once ached with grief and hatred now began to reach out in forgiveness. His attitude toward himself, his people, and even his people's enemies radically changed. Now he is committed to a ministry of reconciliation between Palestinians and Israelis.

This kind of thorough transformation isn't humanly possible. Only God can bring it about. And He can bring it about in our lives as well, from the moment of our conversion to Christ.

THE ADVENTURE: A BEGINNING STEP

Do you remember when you first came to Christ? Perhaps it was a climactic event, now firmly etched in your memory. Or maybe it gradually dawned on you after months or years of seeking: "Yes, I *do* believe after all!"

However it has come about, our conversion to Christ is only the beginning step of a lifetime adventure with God. It is not the finale but the prelude to what God has in store for us. For the seed that is planted in good soil not only produces a crop, it yields an abundant harvest, vastly multiplying itself. This imagery refers to the rich results when a receptive soul encounters the Word of God. The Bible is able to do more than produce change here and there in us. It has the power to transform our entire being into a constantly blossoming garden of new life. The Christian life, in other words, is not just a state of being; conversion initiates a lifetime process of growth.

But what does it really mean, in practical terms, to grow as a Christian? It means to become more and more like God intends us to be. He created us His image-bearers reflecting His glory (see Genesis 1:26-27), but sin has tarnished that image and degraded the glory. This sounds rather abstract until we realize that God has given us a flesh-and-blood model of what we should be like. Christian growth means to become more and more like Jesus.

> For those God foreknew He also predestined to be conformed to the likeness of His Son, that He might be the firstborn among many brothers. (Romans 8:29)

Because we need to know *how* to grow in the character of Christ, God draws us to the pages of the Bible. After all, who but the Father Himself can tell His children how to live in ways that free them in spirit, so they move from pleasing themselves to pleasing Him? The Bible is therefore, the bedrock for spiritual growth, a divinely given resource for positive change in our lives.

Clearly, books have the power to transform those who read them. A gripping novel can give its readers new goals, new perspectives, new priorities. The Bible is a book and, thus, also has transforming power. But it offers riches far more valuable than the insights of any other writings. Breathed out by the living God, its inspired words reach down to the very core of our being. Augustine eventually said it this way: "I have read in Plato and Cicero sayings that are very wise and very beautiful; but I never read in either of them 'Come unto me all ye that labor and are heavy laden.'"[2]

THE CHALLENGE: A WILLING RESPONSE

In a sense, all of us labor and are heavy laden today. If you were to look into your heart at this moment, what heavy burdens would you name? What load of concern would flow into your mind, the daily weight that feels like a sentence to hard labor? Christian writer Paul Little once described the burden as "that cold-mashed-potatoes feeling that comes when you wake up and begin to remember all your problems"[3]

Many of us wake up to those potatoes each morning, and the invitation of Jesus is for all of us: "Come unto Me." And happily, we can respond to Him because of the Book that conveys His bidding with such power and hope. I can testify to what happens when any ordinary person opens to that gentle calling because I have felt the power of the Word at work in my own life. For example, among many other failings, I hate verbal and emotional conflict. If a student comes to my office and says, "I don't understand why you gave me a C-. It's not fair!" I'll see the potential for argument and cringe internally. Yes, I know the conflict will only intensify through my avoidance. And this weakness in my character has led to problems in my friendships, in my marriage, and in my approach to parenting.

I have avoided conflict because at some fundamental level I have picked up the idea that it is wrong, and it makes me feel guilty and nervous when I engage in it. However, as I have read the Bible, I have learned by its teaching and example that conflict is not a sin. Imagine being there, for instance, when Jesus knotted together a whip and started tossing money changers out of the temple courts. No conflict-avoidance there! Slowly and imperfectly I have learned from the Bible the virtue of a boldness that loves others by honestly dealing with my concerns and theirs. This change has strengthened all my relationships.

No, the Bible is not just like any other book; it uncovers our lives and exposes the inner core. In one of a number of self-reflective comments, the Bible describes its life-changing force as a sword:

> For the word of God is living and active. Sharper than any double-edged sword, it penetrates even to dividing soul and spirit, joints and marrow; it judges the thoughts and attitudes of the heart. (Hebrews 4:12)

The sword speaks of the Bible's cutting-edge ability to get under our skin. God uses the Bible to slice into us, to pierce our lives for positive change. What does that mean to you? As you search the inner recesses of your life, where are the places of hurt that might benefit from a holy blade lancing long-infected wounds?

And what forces within you might be resisting such merciful, painful surgery?

As children, we often don't like the foods we need for full growth and health. So it is with spiritual food. While on one level we desire change, on another we are afraid of the transformation that reading the Bible may bring about. Our task is to bring those fears before the Book and its Author. As anxious fawns approaching a quiet pond of water—wide-eyed, ears attentive—we can creep up to the waters of life. "Come, drink up my goodness into your soul," says Jesus, for here, in the Word, is where we take on the likeness of Christ—a transformation from death to life, from meaninglessness to real and lasting purpose, from sadness to joy.

Theologian Karl Barth described how excitement for reading the Bible can grow this way: it is like looking out a window and seeing people standing on the street, holding up their hands to shade their eyes. They gaze up into the sky and point to something they cannot yet see, for the overhang of the roof prevents their view, but they are truly excited. Something is happening, or about to happen, and as we observe, we pick up the excitement, too. The mystery of it captures us, and our curiosity keeps our faces pressed to the window. No doubt something incredibly important is about to happen . . .[4]

That is the intrigue of picking up the Bible. And actually, if we could only see it, what is always "happening," every moment of the day, is the love of God searching us out. "It is love that asks," said Augustine in his later years, "that seeks, that knocks, that finds, and that is faithful to what it finds."[5] And that love shines through clearly in God's gracious decision to give us His Word, to tell us exactly how much He cares for us and what He plans to make of us.

> Dear friends, now we are children of God, and what we
> will be has not yet been made known. But we know that
> when he appears, we shall be like him, for we shall see
> him as he is. (1 John 3:2)

To grow into His likeness, however, we need to be willing to see who we are right now. We need to look inside to see what is good and needs to be encouraged. We'll discover as well what is self-destructive, leading us away from God and His love. As we shall see, the Bible is not only a potent seed that leads to growth but a brilliant mirror of our souls.

2
THE MIRROR
OF OUR SOULS

Seong Hyun woke up with a stomachache. He had been out with his college roommates partying most of the night, but this dull pain in his stomach was far more than a reminder of his late-night drinking. It was the ache of emptiness. As he rummaged through the pile of clothes on his dresser, he caught a glimpse of his haggard face in the mirror. These parties are getting old, he thought. They used to be fun, but they're definitely losing their attraction.

It was getting tougher to motivate himself for school-work. Class in five minutes! He pulled on a wrinkled T-shirt and contemplated the little ketchup stain on the left sleeve. *What am I really working for, anyway? Jobs are scarce, and even if I get one, what do I really want to accomplish in life?*

He grabbed his books and stumbled out the door into sunlight that hurt his eyes. *Soon—real soon—I've got to figure out who I am and what in the world I'm supposed to be doing . . .*

FACING THE HOLY MIRROR

Novelist James A. Michener once said: "If a man happens to find himself, he has a mansion which he can inhabit with dignity all the days of his life." We are all in the process of "finding ourselves" throughout our life journey. But sometimes the quest is more apparent to us than at other times. When has it seemed most urgent for you: During the college years? When starting a family? Approaching middle age? Sometimes we are thoroughly intentional about this search. At other times, we push the big questions to the back burner while more practical concerns take up our immediate attention. But in some way, especially in the important decisions we make, we are always asking: *Who am I? Why am I here?*

So how can we get deep insight into our identity? Where do we go to see a true reflection of who we are? Anyone who reads the papers or watches the nightly news knows that our society no longer has a single overarching worldview holding it together. Diversity is healthy and can be good, but it also leads to an alienating fragmentation when God is left out of the picture. With our society's loss of connection to God over the years, we've lost an understanding of ourselves as God's creatures. We are left with the question, "Are we the gods of the universe or just the sludge of the earth?"

Even Christians with strong faith in God live in this society and are bombarded by alien moral standards and conflicting worldviews. As we approach the year 2000, society continues to embrace the diversity and fragmentation that has resulted in this lack of connection to our true Source.

Also, our lives are pulled in countless directions. We face so many options for work, leisure, education, and relationships that we can have trouble making decisions—or even paying attention.

Survival will be difficult in this so-called postmodern world if our society can find no philosophical cord to bind life together and give it meaning. No one escapes the demands of choice, but on what grounds will choices be made? No one escapes the pain of life, but how is one to cope with that pain?

Every morning I get up and brush my teeth. Unfortunately, the mirror stands over the sink, and I am forced to take a look at myself after a night's sleep. Just as a mirror reflects how we look physically, the Bible is a mirror of our souls. Referring to the book of Psalms, John Calvin said,

> What various and resplendent riches are contained in
> this treasure, it were difficult to find words to describe . . .
> I have been wont to call this book not inappropriately, an
> anatomy of all parts of the soul; for there is not an emo-
> tion of which anyone can be conscious that is not here
> represented as in a mirror.[1]

Calvin elsewhere applied his mirror metaphor not just to the Psalms but to the entire Bible. What did he mean by it? He rightly believed that when we read the Bible something reflective happens, just like what goes on in the morning as we stand before the mirror. However, instead of getting a good look at our bodies, we get a glimpse of what is going inside of us. Left to our own devices, we are lost, searching for our "true selves" in places that could never yield success. But the Bible articulates what is going on inside of us—tells the story of our lives—and ministers to our needs, our guilt, and our alienation.

The divine story of the Bible has much to say about our own life stories. Indeed, as we look back into our past, we see that our journey has a plot like a book. As we read the Scriptures we see how the divine story illuminates that plot in the light of God's will for us.

Take the case of Sam and Mary, for example. They struggled with their life situation. They didn't have anything of their own. Sam couldn't find a job and Mary worked as a dishwasher in a local cafe owned by a godless man who constantly exploited his employees. Mary's parents let them use a spare bedroom in their house, but this created even more tension in both families.

Sam and Mary were Christians who truly pursued God, but God often seemed absent. They wanted to start a family but worried they wouldn't be able to afford the expense that comes with children. They had enough to eat, and that was about it. In a sense, they wondered what good their faith was. Would things really be any worse if they simply gave up on God?

But one day in their daily devotions they stumbled across Psalm 73:

> But as for me, my feet had almost slipped;
>   I had nearly lost my foothold.
> For I envied the arrogant

> when I saw the prosperity of the wicked.
> They have no struggles;
>> their bodies are healthy and strong.
> They are free from the burdens common to man;
>> they are not plagued by human ills. (verses 2-5)

Here is what they had been thinking all along! The psalmist perfectly expressed their anguish. To him, too, it seemed that the godless prospered while those who followed God languished. The psalmist became their voice of fear and anger. But just as the psalmist's story became their own, he pointed them toward God. After reflection, the psalmist realized:

> Surely you place them on slippery ground;
> you cast them down to ruin. . . .
> Yet I am always with you;
> you hold me by my right hand. (verses 18, 23)

In a word, this psalm-as-a-mirror articulated Sam and Mary's struggles and helped them face their present circumstances by giving them hope for the future. The psalm also acted as a seed in their lives, taking root in several directions. In the first place, they began to lose their feeling of panic, the sense that God was not in control. They began to see that difficult situations weren't the result of evil overwhelming good as they stood by helplessly. Rather, God's good gifts consisted of more than the material things available in this world; His greatest good gift was Himself. This perspective gave them a new peace and confidence. They no longer looked down on themselves, but began to face the future with boldness.

None of this happened by magic; it was natural that the Father's Word should work in His children's lives this way. As writer Alan Jones put it:

> The Bible is important for the believing community, not as
> an oracle or magic formula, but as the document that
> bears witness to fundamental experience without which its
> members cannot understand themselves and their world.
> Everyone has such a document or collection of texts. They
> are often an unacknowledged anthology of readings, experiences, and events that have been stuck together with
> scissors and paste. The point is that everyone lives from

some sort of "text" or "script." The Bible is the major text of Christians. It provides the architecture of our thoughts.[2]

The Bible helps us understand ourselves in the midst of our confusion, gives us an architectural structure for our thinking, and ministers to us by pointing us to God. We read the Scriptures and see inside ourselves. All of this is why we can say that the Bible is a mirror to our souls.

ADDRESSING THE WHOLE PERSON

But what do we mean by the "soul," and how does the Bible talk about it? The term *soul* is making a comeback in our day, along with *angels*. A hunger permeates our society: people are open to spiritual realities as they have not been in many years. Indeed, some of the best-selling books of the past few years, even in the nonreligious market, have the word *soul* in their titles, for example, *Chicken Soup for the Soul*.

But what exactly is a soul? Much of the contemporary discussion has been vague, capitalizing on people's overwhelming desire for something more than a purely material existence. People often think of the soul as an entity separate from the body or as some good, religious aspect of our personality that is somehow separate from the less savory parts of us.

The biblical use of the term *soul* is much different from this, however. In the Bible, *soul* refers to the whole person, emphasizing what is at our core and what makes us tick. Indeed, the soul is not seen as separate from the body at all; the Bible recognizes us as complex beings that are neither merely defined *by* our physical substance nor *apart* from it.

The Bible, as a mirror of the soul, addresses our whole being, penetrating beyond surface realities to get to the heart of what we think, feel, desire, and decide. Understanding this emphasis is crucial, or we open the Bible expecting that its main purpose will be merely to inform our intellect, to tell us who God is and what our relationship with Him is all about. Don't misunderstand. The Bible *is* a book that feeds our intellect, but it does far, far more than that. It arouses our emotions, stimulates our imagination, and appeals to our will. The Bible addresses us as whole people, and that is why we must come to it with our hearts—in order to experience it.

The secret and reality of this blissful life in God cannot be understood without receiving, living, and experiencing it.

If we try to understand it only with the intellect, we will find our effort useless. A scientist had a bird in his hand. He saw that it had life, and, wanting to find out in what part of the bird's body the life was, he began dissecting the bird. The result was that the very life of which he was in search disappeared mysteriously. Those who try to understand the inner life merely intellectually will meet with a similar failure. The life for which they are looking will vanish in the analysis.[3]

The Bible draws us in — to real life and full personhood. Therefore, true spirituality does not lead to an anemic, "other worldly" attitude toward life but an enjoyment of God's good gifts here on earth as a down payment on eternal joy in heaven.

For example, let's look at how the Bible addresses sexuality. A person with a distorted view of spirituality might recoil from sex as something that is sinful, tying us to the material (or "the flesh," which would be considered bad). But true spirituality, informed by the Word of God, leads to proper enjoyment of sexual pleasure. For we have been created with all of our intense desire. Have you noticed it? It's a longing on many levels, and the sexual longing is one aspect of our creaturehood, placed there by God. The Scriptures lead us to recognize that all of our desires are, at bottom, a longing for God, and they will lead us to Him if we let them. Even the pleasure of sex can serve that purpose when it is used as God intended.

Since God wants to address our whole person, He chose a medium that would inform our intellect, fire our imaginations, fuel our emotions, and guide our behavior. So, with regard to sexuality, God has given us the Song of Songs, a powerful and erotic love poem.

SEIZING THE IMAGINATION

Exactly how does the Bible address the whole person? How does it penetrate our souls? It speaks powerfully and intimately through stories and poetry.

Consider the form in which God has chosen to give us His Word. Have you noticed that the Bible isn't a philosophical treatise or a systematic theology? God certainly could have chosen these forms to tell us about Himself, and if the Bible were exclusively or even primarily interested in informing our intellect, this would be a magnificent way to communicate with His people. But the Bible isn't a compendium of philosophical or theological essays. There is certainly nothing wrong with philosophy and theology. Indeed, in the right context, they are extremely helpful. But they can be too abstract, too impersonal.

Also notice that the Bible is not a confession of faith. Many Christians and many faithful denominations have confessions of faith and catechisms through which they express what they believe the Bible teaches. These are excellent ways of summarizing the content of the Bible, affirming the important truths it teaches, and defining who we are as Christians. Once again, God could have chosen to tell us about Himself through catechism and confession, but He wisely decided not to.

Our faith is grounded in historical events which took place in space and time (see 1 Corinthians 15:14). Therefore, God could have written a history textbook to tell us about His plan of salvation. But once again, He did not. God wisely and compassionately chose to reveal Himself to His people through stories and poems.

Instead of systematic theology and abstract philosophy, we have the Psalms and the letters of Paul. Instead of an objective, scientific history textbook, we have the stories of David and Goliath, Samson and Delilah.

To say that the Bible comes to us as stories and poems does not mean that biblical events are mythological or historically untrue. No, these stories accurately tell us what actually happened. But they do so in a gripping, vivid style that keeps us on the edge of our seats. And they do it in a manner that celebrates God and His ways in the world.

As such, the Bible speaks to the whole person. Its stories seize our imaginations. Its poems pluck at our heartstrings. The events and images do more than simply inform us; they suck us into the "story" of our God, bringing us into His life. And none of this will let go of us until we are changed people.

BRINGING OUR STORIES TO HIS STORY

God intends to change us through His Word. He thus speaks to us in a way that captures our hearts and draws them close to His heart.

> Every one of us has had experiences which we have not been able to explain: a sudden sense of loneliness or a feeling of wonder or awe in the face of the universal vastness. Or we have had a fleeting visitation of light like an illumination from some other sun, giving us in a quick flash an assurance that we are from another world, that our origins are divine . . . We were forced to suspend our acquired

doubts while, for a moment, the clouds were rolled back and we saw and heard for ourselves.[4]

What similar experiences in your life would you name as conveying the transcendent? The stories of the Bible "roll back the clouds" on all such moments, providing an immediate connection between God's awesomeness and our own lives. In this sense, our "stories" come together. For, as we have said, our lives are stories. When we meet new people, and they ask us to tell them about ourselves, we tell them stories. And the Bible invites us to bring our own story to its story. It compels us to understand our story in the light of the great story of God's dealings with the world.

So what is your story? Imagine telling it to someone, perhaps a child. What would be the beginning, the main plot, the potential endings? Who are the characters and their primary motivations? If you have a little time to think about these things right now, try rehearsing your story during a few moments of quiet reflection. You might even jot down a few of the major events and themes, as you reflect on these questions in the days ahead:

- How has the Bible shed light on my story? What stories and poetry in the Bible most directly reflect what my life is all about?
- How have I reacted and responded to my losses? My joys? My successes? What insights about who I am and where I'm going have come through in the tough times? In the good times?
- What would I say has been the direction and purpose of my life as I look backward and forward? Where do I see the hand of God at work? When has God seemed most real and close? Most absent or enigmatic?
- How is my life "making sense" so far? What are the most confusing aspects of my story so far? In what ways is the Bible a mirror of what has happened and what is happening?
- What "big questions" have I been asking over the course of my life? To what extent have they been answered? How would I rate the process—and quality—of my decision making? To what degree have biblical principles informed my choices?
- What have been my deepest desires? How have they

been fulfilled? What still awaits fulfillment? What role will God and His Word play in this ongoing quest?

Someone once said, "Before God can deliver us we must undeceive ourselves." This is hard work, but bringing questions like these to the Scriptures moves us toward amazing depths of self-revelation. We *can* undeceive ourselves. That is the adventure we take up, again and again, whenever we come to the Bible with seeking hearts. We are letting God's Spirit work in us to make us a little less false, a little more genuine. If we are open, we will slowly but surely become who we really are in Him.

3
THE SURPRISING ENCOUNTER

"Don't you see, I'm not a fake, not about this." Some people—certain movie fans who flocked to the 1990 blockbuster *Ghost*—may remember that line. It took Whoopi Goldberg, as the phony psychic, quite a while to convince a bereaved woman that her fiancé was trying to communicate with his beloved from beyond the grave.

Why the tough sell? Actually, it would be the same in real life. As much as we might be intrigued by the possibility of disembodied spirits, most of us find it hard to believe in a true-to-life ghost story. It's just a cute, Hollywood fantasy.

FACE-TO-FACE WITH REALITY

Yet people do look for life-changing help from all kinds of so-called spiritual sources. But it is only the Bible that works as a seed to transform our lives and grow the fruit of Christ's character within us. And the Bible is the mirror that shows us what we're truly like at the core of our being. But why, exactly, does the Bible have this extraordinary power?

Because it brings us face-to-face with almighty God.

Do you remember the parable of the rich man and Lazarus in Luke 16:19-31? Through this intriguing story, Jesus tells us that the Bible brings the confused and the hurting into relationship with God Himself:

> "There was a rich man who was dressed in purple and fine linen and lived in luxury every day. At his gate was laid a beggar named Lazarus, covered with sores and longing to eat what fell from the rich man's table. Even the dogs came and licked his sores."

Lazarus and the unnamed rich man represent the classic contrast between those who have much and those who have nothing. But death comes to both the rich and the poor, and so it came to Lazarus and the rich man.

After death, their positions reversed. Lazarus was carried by angels to "Abraham's side," while the rich man remained "in torment." Indeed, it is interesting to note that, though the rich man was well known in life, it is Lazarus the unknown whom we know by name; the rich man is lost in anonymity. The rich man's thirst burned hot and he wanted Lazarus to "dip the tip of his finger in water" in order to cool his tongue. But that would not be allowed.

The man then approached Abraham with a second request. If nothing could be done about his situation, he wanted to warn his five brothers to change their ways and avoid his fate. He asks that he might rise from the dead to go and warn his brothers. The dialogue that follows provides great insight into the crucial role the Bible plays in life:

> "Abraham replied, 'They have Moses and the Prophets; let them listen to them.'
> 'No, father Abraham,' he said, 'but if someone from the dead goes to them, they will repent.'
> "He said to him, 'If they do not listen to Moses and the Prophets, they will not be convinced even if someone rises from the dead.'" (verses 29-31)

How often we think like the rich man! In essence, Jesus tells him that the copy of the Bible his brothers have on their coffee table is more convincing and exciting than the ghost of their dead brother could ever be![1] After all, such an appearance could later be interpreted as a dream or nightmare, or the result of indigestion. But the Bible has always been there to be read, rechecked, pondered, and meditated upon. In other words, the Bible conveys a dose of reality far more potent than any ghost, whether coming from a place of torment or from a Hollywood movie set.

A HEAVENLY INTRUSION

God speaks to us through the Bible. He encounters us in its pages. It is true that He speaks to us in other ways as well but never so clearly and directly as in Scripture. As I look out my window on this beautiful spring day in Philadelphia, I see a reflection of God's care for His people in the sunshine and fresh air. When a devastating storm hits, I see His power. Further, since people we meet are made in God's image, I see a very pale — and indeed distorted — picture of God in them. I can also see such a dim picture in myself. But because of our sin and finitude, which resulted in the fall of all creation, we wouldn't have more than a vague impulse of God if He had not chosen to speak to us in the Bible. It would be like a movie "ghost" trying to make contact with the living but never fully appearing and never actually revealing himself.

But God *has* chosen to reveal Himself to us in the Bible, and it is God's description of Himself. It is not an internal voice that could be the product of our own wish fulfillment; it is the voice of God addressing us from outside of ourselves. In this regard, the Bible is the other side of prayer. I speak to God by praying to Him, and He answers me most clearly as I read the Bible. To pray much but not study the Bible traps us in a one-way conversation with God. Prayer without Bible reading is narcissistic. We hear ourselves but not God.

The Bible is not just another book; it is a voice from outside of us and above us intruding into our lives to give us a better perspective on the issues that confront us daily. From only our limited perspective, we can have no certainty as we look into the future. We can't be certain that we will keep our jobs, our friends, our spouses, our sanity, even our lives. As the author of Ecclesiastes (often called simply, "the Teacher") put it in 9:11, when life is viewed under the sun (that is, from a purely human perspective), "time and chance" rule human destiny.

But the Bible gives us a wisdom from above. Now, of course, it does not give us any false assurances. Indeed, it says that the life of God's people will be characterized by pain and loss, but it also tells us that God is with us in the midst of our pain. It tells us that even in the horrible occurrences of our lives "in all things God works for the good of those who love Him" (Romans 8:28) and that death does not "end it all" but leads to an eternity of bliss.

We desperately need to know these things. Therefore, the Bible is not a dispassionate report to uninterested readers. It goes beyond calmly presenting evidence to a doubting world that God exists and is good. The Bible is passionate, more like preaching than anything else. It urgently proclaims God's message of salvation to a spiritually hungry world. It does not argue for God's existence; it assumes it and points out what this God has done in history to rescue a lost people.

In all of these ways, then, the Bible is God's Word to us. God speaks directly and clearly today in the pages of that ancient book. Nothing else compares with it. If we want to talk with God, we must turn to the Bible, for that is where we will meet Him.

A GOD OF RELATIONSHIP

Of course, any Bible itself *is* "just a book," ink on a page. And we do not change because we have a relationship with a book. We change through a relationship with a person—God Himself. This is why the Bible has a life-giving quality. When we go to the Bible to encounter God, what we find surprises us. We encounter something far more compelling than an arid theology or philosophy. We feel the grasp of a warm hand in ours.

For some reason, Christians, whether in the pulpit or in conversation, tend to talk about God in the abstract. God is powerful, good, and wise. He is infinite and eternal. He is holy and just. The Bible certainly uses this language, and we can too. But as we read through the Bible, we see that God prefers to talk about Himself in concrete images. He is a shepherd, a king, a warrior, a parent, a wisdom teacher, a spouse. We might say that *God's primary way of revealing Himself is through picture images of relationship.* God wants to tell us who He is, and He does so by comparing Himself to people and things we know well.

For instance, the people of Israel, for whom Psalm 23 was first written, had frequent contact with shepherds; many of them *were* shepherds. So the psalmist invited them to consider how God was like a shepherd. Certainly, they readily recognized how God differed from the human shepherds they knew: not all were reliable; some were likely despicable human beings.

But the psalmist used this image to teach us about God's protection and His guidance of His people, who are His "sheep." The Israelites would be aware that human shepherds take great risks to keep their charges from danger and wild animals. This word picture not only increased their understanding of who God was, but also elicited a warm emotional response in a way that a straightforward prose description would not.

Consider another example: God is King (see Exodus 15:18; Deuteronomy 33:5; Psalms 47, 93, 96, 98, 100). The Israelites, again the original hearers of these passages, knew what a king was. The king was an absolute sovereign who guided the whole community and had the power of life and death over his subjects. No one could get in the way of the king. That was what God was like, too. But God, rather than being the king of a mere nation, was the ruler of the universe.

The biblical images for God are numerous. We couldn't even scratch the surface in describing them in this book. However, we can spend a moment reflecting on why God has chosen to reveal Himself to us in this way. First, as we have already seen, picture images are concrete and vivid, communicating to everyone, not just to an intellectual elite. Everyone knew something about kings, soldiers, shepherds, parents, and husbands. So when God spoke of Himself in these ways, His hearers had a frame of reference for their understanding.

Second, images speak to the soul, to the whole person, and not just to the mind. Images not only inform us about who God is, they stimulate our imaginations as we contemplate how God is like His earthly counterparts and how He differs from them. Our emotions thrill as we stand before a masterpiece of color at the art museum. The reds and blues and yellows reach into us and catch us up into a few moments of other-worldly connection. That is the power of an image, and our whole selves are drawn toward God in just this way. Perhaps this soul connection is why the Bible so often refers to God as Father. Whether our experience of an earthly father has been positive or painful, we all have a heartfelt yearning to know what it would mean to relate to a perfectly good, kind, and loving parent.

Seeing God as parent may seem childish. But might there be, in the unadmitted sparkle of the child within you, a sometime longing to climb into God's fatherly lap, to nestle against God's motherly breast, to rest for a moment in the shadow of God's wings, or to be held in God's strong and tender arms? If you could allow yourself to feel it, are there not times when you would love to cry on God's shoulder, to let God tell you that you are worthwhile and beautiful? And is there not something in you that would be delighted if you could bring a smile to God's face?[2]

Have you let the Bible speak to your soul lately by climbing into God's lap through its pages?

A third reason the Bible uses imagery for God is that word pictures preserve the divine mystery. We have already observed that an image brings together two things that are different in many ways in order to emphasize a core similarity. But the comparison is left to us and not precisely spelled out.

When do we go too far in pressing the similarity? When not far enough? This is a question that frustrates the prosaic minds among us because we can never precisely draw the line.

As humans, we are caught between necessity and idolatry. We need our words and images if we are to talk with each other about God. But when talking about God, let us proceed with caution, removing our shoes, lest we succeed only in creating a god who is not God at all.[3]

The ambiguity of biblical imagery preserves the inscrutable mystery surrounding God. He is knowable, because He chooses to reveal Himself to us. But He is ultimately incomprehensible. That means we can adequately, but not exhaustively, know God. He goes beyond the capacity of our finite minds. Thus, through the use of metaphors and other images, God both reveals and conceals Himself from us.

Before we leave this topic, let me emphasize again that the most pervasive images found in the Bible are word pictures of relationship. (Sure, some are not. God is a rock, a fortress, a light.) The most widely and repetitively used images convey relationship. So when we think of God as Shepherd, we remember we are His sheep. We are the soldiers in His army. We are the Father's children. We are the subjects of our King.

Take a moment, then, to consider your own "picture" of God. If you can be still and calm for a moment, take some time to be in God's presence. What images arise? What feelings? What sense of who

God is? I'm hoping that many of the images and pictures that come to mind serve to embrace you in the love and goodness and grace of God; for what we find in Scripture is a God who speaks to us in a language that knocks at our heart's door—that of metaphor—and invites us into fellowship with Him.

So far, however, we have not approached the primary way that God speaks to us in order to draw us into relationship. Ultimately He uses the best "imagery" of all—a living, breathing human being.

CHRIST—THE CENTER OF SCRIPTURE

The message of the Bible concerns a people gone awry. God created men and women, but they turned against Him and broke the relationship. He could have justly given up on His creatures, but He did not. Instead, He pursues them. The Bible is the story of the rescue of God's lost people.

That story climaxes in Jesus Christ. The gospel of John gets right to the point in the first chapter when the apostle proclaims that "the Word became flesh and made His dwelling among us" (John 1:14), so that anyone who believed in Him became "children of God" (verse 12).

We can, therefore, understand why Christians tend to spend most of their Bible-reading time in the New Testament. Jesus has come; He supersedes the prophets, according to Hebrews 1:1-2:

> In the past God spoke to our forefathers through the
> prophets at many times and in various ways, but in these
> last days he has spoken to us by his Son, whom he
> appointed heir of all things, and through whom he made
> the universe.

"Why bother with the Old Testament?" Few Christians would put it so blatantly. They simply vote with their time by only rarely reading the Old Testament. After all, according to Jesus, the *whole* Bible, Old Testament included, is about Him. Remember His conversation with the two disciples on the road to Emmaus? It is after His resurrection but before He appeared to anyone else. The disciples wonder why Jesus had to die. Jesus looks at them in amazement and says:

> "How foolish you are, and how slow of heart to believe all
> that the prophets have spoken! Did not the Christ have to
> suffer these things and then enter his glory?" And beginning

with Moses and all the Prophets, he explained to them
what was said in all the Scriptures concerning himself.
(Luke 24:25-27)

And then not long after this meeting, Jesus appears to others of
His disciples and tells them:

"This is what I told you while I was still with you: Everything
must be fulfilled that is written about me in the Law of
Moses, the Prophets and the Psalms." (24:44)

Jesus here refers to His Bible as "Moses and all the Prophets" and
then "the Law of Moses, the Prophets and the Psalms." Since there
was not yet a *New* Testament, Jesus could not refer to the *Old* Testament. Instead, He uses the language that was familiar to His Jewish
audience in the first century A.D. Genesis through Deuteronomy
was referred to as the "Law" or "Moses." The rest of what we call the
Old Testament was either lumped together as the "Prophets" or
divided into two parts, the "Prophets" and the "Writings." Jesus here
refers to the Writings as "the Psalms," which was the first book of that
third section.

Jesus is saying that the whole Bible anticipated His coming suffering and glorification in such a way that His followers should not
have been surprised by what happened on Calvary or afterwards.
His words have tremendous implications for how we understand the
Bible. We already know that the Gospels and Epistles speak of Jesus,
but now we realize that the history, poetry, law, and prophets of the
Old Testament do so, too.

The way Jesus speaks of the Old Testament corrects a mistake we
might make as we come to the Scriptures. Many might think, "Sure,
I know that the Old Testament speaks of Christ. I have read Isaiah 9,
11, and 53. I know the messianic psalms (2, 16, 22, 69, 110). I've discovered a number of startling predictions of Christ." But Jesus here
says that *all the Scriptures* concerned Himself. It is not just a few Old
Testament passages that teach us about Him but every bit of the
sacred writings. We should never read or teach from the Old Testament without asking how Jesus is anticipated in it.

Augustine recognized this truth and coined a phrase that many
Christians still appreciate. This fourth-century church father said that "the
New Testament is in the Old concealed, and the Old is in the New
revealed." As we will see, this does not mean we'll adopt a "secret" method

of interpretation that attempts to unlock hidden prophecies in every verse. Some have used the Christocentric nature of the Bible to read things into the text that are not there. But once we have the big picture, we will see how naturally the Old Testament presents Jesus to us.

For Jesus is the whole point. No matter how much we love the pages of Scripture, we must keep in mind that it is the Christ of Scripture who claims our deepest affection. Otherwise, the Bible could become a thing of worship in itself.

> Evangelical Christians are not, or ought not to be, what we are sometimes accused of being, namely, "bibliolaters," worshipers of the Bible. We do not worship the Bible; we worship the Christ of the Bible.
>
> Here is a young man who is in love. He has a girlfriend who has captured his heart. As a result he carries a photograph of his beloved in his wallet because it reminds him of her when she is far away. Sometimes, when nobody is looking, he might even take the photograph out and give it a surreptitious kiss. But kissing the photograph is a poor substitute for the real thing. And so it is with the Bible. We love it only because we love him of whom it speaks. [4]

So far in the first section of this book, we have set the foundation for a proper reading of the Bible by speaking of its transforming power. We now know *why* the Bible ignites the character of Christ in us: it is a seed that grows fruit in us; it is a mirror that reveals our souls to us. And it is a word in which we encounter our risen Lord.

How Do *You* Encounter Him?

"We should be as careful of the books we read, as of the company we keep," said writer Tyron Edwards. "The dead very often have more power than the living."

All the books ever written were penned by men and women who have died or will die. But Jesus, center of Scripture, lives within us. It remains for us to open up to Him and become aware of His presence each moment, to be present for Him throughout the day.

How does the Bible help us do that? By offering the opportunity to encounter Him in the words and events that flow to us from the sacred pages. Why not take a few minutes right now to see how this can work in your life? Choose any portion of the Scripture, preferably starting with a reading that has a sense of "place" to it. Then put yourself into the scene. For example, try reading John 21:4-13 with this approach, being there on the shore with Jesus.

> Early in the morning, Jesus stood on the shore, but the disciples did not realize that it was Jesus.
> He called out to them, "Friends, haven't you any fish?"
> "No," they answered.
> He said, "Throw your net on the right side of the boat and you will find some." When they did, they were unable to haul the net in because of the large number of fish. Then the disciple whom Jesus loved said to Peter, "It is the Lord!" As soon as Simon Peter heard him say, "It is the Lord," he wrapped his outer garment around him (for he had taken it off) and jumped into the water. The other disciples followed in the boat, towing the net full of fish, for they were not far from shore, about a hundred yards. When they landed, they saw a fire of burning coals there with fish on it, and some bread.
> Jesus said to them, "Bring some of the fish you have just caught."
> Simon Peter climbed aboard and dragged the net ashore. It was full of large fish, 153, but even with so many, the net was not torn. Jesus said to them, "Come and have breakfast." None of the disciples dared ask him, "Who are you?" They knew it was the Lord. Jesus came, took the bread and gave it to them, and did the same with the fish.

In silent meditation, consider: what does the Man look like as He stands in the early morning sun? Can you see the glinting of light in His hair and beard? What is in His eyes? They are focused on you! Feel the love in Him, extending to you, His disciple. When He calls out, how does His voice sound? Take a moment to hear—really hear with your heart—as He calls you "Friend." Bask in the goodness of being a beloved friend of the Lord.

Hear the water lapping at the sides of the boat. Take in the smell of rotting nets and the pungent odors of fish and tackle. Acknowledge the willingness of this King to be immersed in the mundane world of business. What is He like at your own place of work? How does He care for you there and help you with your daily catch? Let Him bless you in your work right now.

Are you sleepy? But then how do you feel as you suddenly

recognize: it is the Lord! What is it like to recognize His presence, right now, as you sit in your chair? He is here. It is, indeed, the Lord waiting for you.

As the boat docks and you move across the sand to meet Him, feel the little stones between your toes and approach Him slowly. For here is the love of your life. And He is cooking breakfast for you! Smell the burning coals and let Him serve you. As He passes you a piece of fish, what do you say? What is the silence saying, right now, as you wait before Him—the One who loves you and serves you and calls you to win and serve others?

Though dead, He has returned but not as a ghost. He is a living friend to know forever. Enjoy your fellowship with Him in this precious moment with the Word.

PART II

THE
RECEPTIVE
HEART

4
A Matter of Perspective

Is that a person standing over there by the wall . . . or a tree?

And what does that road sign say: Merge Left . . . or Dead End ahead?

Has it ever happened to you? Maybe you are blessed with excellent vision, but every few years I notice that my eyesight is getting worse. My old glasses just aren't doing the job anymore. My friends start looking like interesting additions to the landscaping, and a routine drive through town becomes a heart-pounding adventure.

So I go to the doctor for a new set of lenses. Suddenly my misty world clears up. And when I walk out to the street in the morning, I can tell the difference between my car and the garbage truck!

THE LENSES THROUGH WHICH WE READ

Yes, I'm exaggerating—to make a point. One of the first lessons young Christians receive is to be careful not to read their own ideas into the Bible. Clearly, this is good advice; we ought to be fully aware of our preconceived ideas and conditions as we approach the text. Nonetheless, this kind of advice can go too far, suggesting that in order to avoid misinterpreting the Bible we must be thoroughly objective, ridding ourselves of our personal desires, interests, and backgrounds. In this view, such subjective aspects of ourselves would work like a bad pair of prescription glasses—with lenses that don't clear up misty vision but rather distort the view.

Yet who can come to the Bible with complete objectivity? Each of us already has built-in lenses through which we interpret things—God's Word included. It is impossible to approach the Bible without personal involvement because we cannot simply throw off our personality, culture, and education as we read the Scriptures. After all, the Bible isn't a frog to be dissected and studied in a sterile laboratory; it is the Word of God which addresses each one-of-a-kind heart and mind. Since the Word is the place where each person meets and experiences the Lord in his own life, we read the Bible through our life experiences, which are legitimate interpretive lenses.

We look at the Bible through "lenses" because we are finite creatures. To be *truly* objective, we would have to be all knowing in a way that only God is. We are restricted to our own culture, education, upbringing, denominational connections, limited teaching on the Bible, economic stratum, and so forth. *Everything that makes us who we are as individual human beings influences us as we read the Bible.* No matter how hard we try, we cannot become completely blank slates with the hope that we will understand the Bible in a thoroughly detached way. There is no escape from looking at the Bible through our built-in lenses.

At Westminster Theological Seminary where I teach the Old Testament, I see this principle at work every day. While many who come to our seminary are Presbyterian in their basic theology, a minority of students come from Baptist, Episcopalian, charismatic, and other denominational backgrounds. Currently, we have students from thirty-five different countries as well. Our 600-member student body consists of men and women, rich and poor, bright and not-so-bright, stable and unstable, single and married. Some are right out of college, others are in their sixties.

These factors and the experiences of my students and myself influence how each of us reads the Bible. Our backgrounds and present concerns don't determine the *meaning* of the Bible, but they do impact how we read it. A Christian from a Latin American barrio, whose government oppresses the poor, will read Psalm 113 with a different emphasis than an upper-class Caucasian American who is fairly satisfied with his living conditions.

Some people feel uncomfortable acknowledging that our lenses influence our interpretation of the Bible and for a good reason. It may be that our lenses aren't helping us interpret the Bible; they may be distorting our understanding of it. We do want to know what the Word of God says to us, but we do not want to improperly impose our perspectives on the Bible.

This danger, as we all know, is quite real. How often have we seen or heard of people who bend the Bible to fit their own needs? That poor Latin American Christian may use her preunderstanding of the Bible to justify rallying the church to revolt against her government. The rich American may use the Bible's teaching on God's blessings to justify his oppression of others as he amasses more wealth. Someone who mercilessly beats his young son might justify his actions on the basis of Proverbs 13:24. A demented cult leader may read biblical prophecy in such a way that he leads his followers to a fiery death.

SOME DISTORTING LENSES

We must become aware of our lenses in order to know whether they help us or hinder us as we listen to God's voice in the Bible. No lens is perfect. Everyone's view of the Bible can be improved and expanded. But the sad truth is that some lenses do hinder more than help, distorting the Bible to an intolerable point. They don't help us see reality clearly at all because they are like spectacles with plain glass in them—merely giving the pretense of help.

Let us survey some common examples of the lenses we ought never to put on. They will cause us to view the Bible as:

A treasure chest of golden truths. The alarm clock rang at 6 A.M., and Kanisha sprang out of bed. Early morning was her favorite time of day. She just couldn't understand people who had to drag themselves out of bed in the morning. After brushing her teeth and showering, she grabbed her Bible and got into her comfortable "praying chair." She closed her eyes and, with a short prayer for guidance, pointed and read:

> I will maintain my righteousness and never let go of it;
> my conscience will not reproach me as long as I
> live. (Job 27:6)

Wow! she thought to herself. *God really can speak to my heart. How did He know that I felt so guilty about that argument with my mother on the phone last night? Well, according to God, I guess I shouldn't let it bother me. It's all behind me now.* She closed the Bible and grabbed her coat, rejoicing that she had completed her Bible study this morning.

Some people, like Kanisha, approach the Bible as a loose collection of inspiring phrases, golden nuggets that fall out of the sky. These ancient sayings lift us up in the morning and help us get through a tough day. But the Bible is certainly more than a collection of mottoes to be framed and placed on the wall of our minds. The Bible is the story of God's salvation and along with the uplifting verses are some pretty hard-hitting statements about humankind and our life in a fallen world. The Bible is a narrative masterpiece, a story made up of many stories. To understand any part we must have a grasp of the whole.

Kanisha's method of choosing a text may not be yours, but have you ever picked up biblical passages as though they were little golden nuggets scattered among other jewels of wisdom? It is a problem of disregarding the broader context. In Kanisha's reading, when Job states the words recorded in 27:6, it is questionable whether Job is as righteous as he thinks he is. Perhaps his conscience *should* have bothered him! In any case, Kanisha improperly applied the verse to her own life without further reflection upon the whole message of the book of Job.

A grab bag of promises and comforts. Gertrude had spent years doing needlepoint, and it lifted her spirit to see all the promises of God so artfully displayed around her house. That was why she felt so comfortable in her warm house and hated to go outside into a rather frightening world.

Another approach to the Bible, similar to the preceding, is one that dips into the Bible only for the comforting promises of God. With this lens on, we see only the things that make us feel better, when, in reality, often the Word of God spoken into our lives ought to make us quite uncomfortable. Yes, there are many, many rich promises in the Bible. But, once again, pulling those promises out of their context means disregarding the totality of the Bible's message.

A compilation of riddles and secrets. The Bible speaks of mysteries, ultimately incomprehensible realities, and the wonder of God and His creation. And this living Word does not submit itself to exhaustive interpretation. Yet the Bible is not a book of riddles for which the interpreter must find a special key to unlock its secrets.

The examples of such an approach are endless. A few years ago I debated a popular radio preacher who felt he had found the key that revealed the true meaning of the Bible. His work was unnecessarily complicated, and it is not worth repeating here, but he felt that much of the Bible pointed to Jesus' return in September 1994. The key, for him, was to apply precise mathematics. In a very convoluted argument, he supposedly demonstrated that God created the world in 11,006 B.C.; therefore, the world must end in 1994. He used passage after passage to buttress his argument, basing everything on the crucial importance of the number thirteen. His faith in this interpretive key was so intense that when 1994 came to a close, he argued that we should follow the calendar of the "Jewish year," which would end in March 1995. That only gave him three months, though, to prolong his inevitable embarrassment.

The Bible is not a book of riddles that needs to be solved. We encounter difficult passages in its pages, but the central message is clear as a bell.

A talisman with magical power. Some people view the Bible as a magical charm to keep close in times of trial or danger. "It's a holy book," said John, "a book that keeps harm at bay and gives me the power to face each day. I take a little Bible with me wherever I go. I heard that a guy once carried a Bible in his breast pocket—and it stopped a bullet. Obviously, the Bible can save your life!"

People who have a view like this read the Bible out of fear. The Bible *can* help prepare us for danger and even death; however, it is primarily a book of *life*. It brings us guidance and encouragement in the face of suffering, but only if we read it, reflect on it, and apply it in practical ways. That is not magic but discipleship.

These are just a few of the ways we try to reduce the Bible to our own size, with lenses that make the Bible smaller than it actually is. Other strategies include treating the Bible like a law book. Or, the opposite, treating it as a book that frees us totally from any rules, arguing that we are in a period of grace in which the law no longer has any role in our lives. Some read the Bible as a political tract, supporting right-wing, Marxist, or feminist agendas.

We must not conclude from these myopic and distorted viewpoints that reading with a perspective is all bad. Even these approaches highlight important truths about the Bible. But they refuse to treat it as an organic whole. And they close off aspects of God and His message that we may not wish to acknowledge.

SOME CHRISTLIKE PERSPECTIVES

To read the Bible through distorting lenses is to blind ourselves to God's full message. The people who use such lenses may not be evil, but they have taken up immature perspectives on Scripture. They grasp a part of the truth about God's Word but then treat it as the most important—or even the only—teaching of the Bible. In contrast, God invites us to come to His Word with commitment and trust, the kind Jesus Himself demonstrated toward His Father's Word. There are certain Christlike perspectives on the Bible that we can embrace in order to read it according to the intention of its divine Author. Consider:

Approaching the Bible as God's Word. Is the Bible the Word of God? Or is it just another inspiring human document? Your answer to this fundamental question will have major impact upon how you read the Bible (and how it "reads" you). Christ Himself affirmed the Scriptures' divine authorship.[1] To accept the Bible as the Word of God is to imitate Christ's own belief and practice.

Along with this fundamental attitude toward the nature of the Bible comes a related question: Do you believe and trust the Bible's view of the universe, that it is more than the material existence we can perceive through our senses? Is there a supernatural dimension to reality, as the Bible describes it?

Our basic view of the nature of the Bible and its world significantly impacts how we read it. The apostle Paul argued,

> If there is no resurrection of the dead, then not even Christ has been raised. And if Christ has not been raised, our preaching is useless and so is your faith. More than that, we are then found to be false witnesses about God, for we have testified about God that he raised Christ from the dead. But he did not raise him if in fact the dead are not raised. For if the dead are not raised, then Christ has not been raised either. And if Christ has not been raised, your faith is futile; you are still in your sins. Then those also who have fallen asleep in Christ are lost. If only for this life we have hope in Christ, we are to be pitied more than all men. (1 Corinthians 15:13-19)

While not speaking directly to our point, Paul draws a close connection between three things: faith (what we believe), the word (his preaching), and the supernatural universe (Christ's resurrection). These three are intertwined and dependent on one another.

The lens that the Bible invites us to put on is a perspective that understands the Bible to be the Word of God. It thus calls us to approach its pages in faith, believing in the universe it describes, even when our senses may not directly confirm what it says. Otherwise, we approach the Bible with skepticism and subject the Bible's worldview to critical analysis rather than letting the Bible analyze every other theory of existence. In an insidious reversal, we become critics of the Bible rather than allowing the Bible to criticize us. Bypassing this unhappy approach, we can bow to the authority of the Bible. Thus, we can let the Lord lead us into His presence, praying as one dedicated noblewoman prayed centuries ago:

Lord, as I read . . .
let me hear you singing.
As I read your words,
let me hear you speaking.
As I reflect on each page,
let me see your image.
And as I seek to put your precepts into practice,
let my heart be filled with joy.[2]

Reading the Bible as a guide for living. We do come to the Bible with certain expectations about its subject matter. Once we accept the Bible as the Word of God we need to ask what God has chosen to speak to us about. Second Timothy 3:16 informs us that God intends to address all of life in His Word:

All Scripture is God-breathed and is useful for teaching, rebuking, correcting and training in righteousness, so that the man of God may be thoroughly equipped for every good work.

Paul encouraged his young mentor, Timothy, to search the Scriptures for answers to life's most perplexing questions. The Bible is our divinely given life guide. Jesus believed this and submitted to His Father's Word for the direction of His life, even to the point of going to the cross.

As we read the Scriptures, we are amazed at how it tells us of life, the whole range of life experiences. It teaches not only about God and our relationship with Him. It instructs us about how to deal with suffering in this world and gives us hope in the midst of everyday chaos. We also receive crucial guidance in marrying, parenting, working, playing, worshiping. The Bible provides the perspective we need in order to live in a way that pleases God in all our endeavors.

Of course, some people take a more academic approach to this passage in Timothy. They argue that here God tells us that the Bible is the *only* place we can learn anything about the world and life. So we must come to the Bible before we address any issue of human concern, whether it be religion, psychology, finance, politics, science, or morality. Others feel that the Bible is only interested in matters of faith. We read the Bible in order to learn about our relationship with God, not to discover the method of creation or to learn of specific developments in ancient history.

As with most controversies, the truth likely dwells between the two positions. Clearly, the Bible is concerned about faith and salvation. But God has accomplished our salvation on earth in real history. Therefore, when the Bible addresses matters of science or history, it speaks *truly* and *accurately*. But often it does not speak *fully*. For instance, we can't find out in the Bible about the best computer software for Bible study. But that doesn't mean computers don't exist or that they shouldn't be in our lives.

Interpreting the Bible with Christlike humility. If anything, the previous paragraphs should lead us to great humility in our interpretation of the Bible. To be sure, a number of basic teachings in the Bible are simply unarguable. The Bible clearly and repetitively teaches that we are sinners in need of a savior. It clearly teaches that the Savior is Jesus Christ. Many, many other fundamental teachings are quite clearly taught in the Bible. However, a number of other teachings are not so clear, including some that are dear to us.

Did God create the universe in six literal days? What about evolution? Will Christ return after, or before, the Rapture? Will there be a thousand-year reign of Christ on earth? These and many other questions of interpretation have caused tremendous fights and rifts down through the centuries. I have definite opinions about them, and, when I first became a Christian, I was willing to go to the wall for them. But now I realize that Christ doesn't want us to fight for interpretations that are neither central to the faith nor capable of absolute certainty. He is growing within each of us a heart that seeks something much better than merely being right.

> Give us a pure heart
> that we may see thee,
> A humble heart
> that we may hear thee,
> A heart of love
> that we may serve thee,
> Thou
> Whom I do not know
> But whose I am.[3]

As Dag Hammarskjold the former General Secretary of the United Nations, expressed in this prayer, we will never have a complete handle on God, never fully "know" Him in this life. All of our theology is finite; only God is infinite. Therefore, as we seek fuller enlightenment about His indescribable character, we'll breed within ourselves a certain humility as we study —that is, we'll wear our interpretive eyeglasses loosely and give our Christian friends the benefit of the doubt and a fair hearing when their interpretations differ from our own.

PROTECTING WHILE PRESERVING

As devoted disciples of Christ, we must develop a recognition that our lenses both help us and can possibly hinder us. We need to wear our lenses, knowing that we approach the text with preunderstanding. But we should wear them lightly, being willing to subject our viewpoints to the Bible itself for correction and change. These are the two poles of reading the Bible with passion, for God desires our hearts to be in pursuit of Him as we read His Word. We cannot be lukewarm, detached, and objective as we read God's Word.

How can we protect ourselves against distorting the Bible while at the same time preserving our passion? First, we'll need to read the whole Bible rather than focusing only on our favorite parts. The Bible teaches its truth repetitively. God comes back again and again to His most important teachings. As we broaden our understanding of the Bible, we will gain more balance in our interpretations. For instance, we'll see that Bible passages promising blessing for the believer are tempered by other passages that acknowledge suffering in a fallen world and the material success of the wicked (see Psalm 73).

Second, as we interpret, we'll need to mentally place ourselves in ancient times, so we can understand the context in which the books of the Bible were written. The books of the Bible were written *directly* to the audiences contemporary to its human authors and only *secondarily* to the generations that followed. As we remember to place ourselves in the ancient world of the Bible, we create a healthy distance between ourselves and the text. (We'll talk more about this later.)

Third, we'll interpret the Bible in community. That doesn't mean I avoid reading the Bible alone in the quiet of my study or bedroom. It means that I should also be talking to other people about my interpretation with an openness to their opinions. I can also read the writings of seasoned Bible scholars from different backgrounds to get their insights on the text. They might see things in the text that I don't. Further reflection may convince me that they are right.

And that is a crucial point. We all look at the Bible through lenses, but we can and often must change "prescriptions." As I read the Bible, I may notice passages that I just can't square with my previous understanding of the text. Perhaps I once thought the Bible taught that women were somehow inferior to men. I read Old Testament laws that seemed to indicate that men were more valuable than women (Leviticus 27:1-10). But by adopting such a position I am forced to struggle with Genesis 1:26-28, which teaches that women, like men, are made in the image of God. I may then have my attention drawn to Galatians 3:28, which says that in Christ there is "neither… male nor female." My understanding of the Bible's teaching on gender may then undergo a major shift that affects not only the way I think but also the way I act.

The moral of the story, then, is that we can change our glasses. We are not imprisoned with a distorted view of the Bible; we can constantly be improving our eyesight. Indeed, most of this book is devoted to helping us discover the best lenses for reading the Scriptures.

Yes, some people are trying to fool themselves that they don't wear glasses at all. This view is dangerous because it doesn't allow a person to be self-critical of his or her preunderstanding. Other people are wearing beaten-up glasses, those big horn-rimmed types with the ear pieces bent out of shape, a bit of masking tape at the nose piece. The lenses haven't been washed for years, and the person who wears them has come to believe that every object he sees is supposed to fade into another. When that happens, so much of God's truth is blocked from view.

We should know that we wear glasses and that our glasses will need adjustment from time to time. That is, we ought to become aware of our subjectivity. As the poet Goethe once said, "Each one sees what he carries in his heart."

5

A Passionate Approach

Ralph was taught in school to read the Bible with a critical eye. He learned that the Bible is like any other book. It's full of mistakes, the typical kinds of mistakes that any human author would make. So instead of submitting himself to the authority of the Word, he submitted the Word to the authority of Ralph. Instead of looking to the Bible for guidance in his daily life, he critiqued it on the basis of what he thought was right and wrong.

And Ralph did have a strong sense of what was right and what was wrong. Some of his Christian friends called it anger, and they tried to show him from the Bible how his attitude was destructive. But he knew better. Sure, he lost some friends and occasionally his marriage was difficult. But he couldn't stand it if people did the wrong thing to him. And since the Bible, for him, was merely a book of religious ideals at best, it didn't help him very much. In Ralph's world of constantly evening the score, "Turn the other cheek" was hardly practical advice.

ENCOURAGING THE SEARCH

If you were Ralph's friend, how would you go about helping him discover the life-transforming power of the Bible?

You might begin by encouraging his spiritual passion. We've seen that reading the Bible with passion means reading with our whole being—intellect, emotions, imagination, and will. It is the opposite of trying to be thoroughly objective or trying to read "without lenses," as Ralph tried to do. That, of course, is impossible.

When we read the Bible, we're called to engage our whole self, submitting ourselves to it in order to meet Jesus, our Lord. "Let the word of Christ dwell in you," said Paul in Colossians 3:16. And our greatest desire should be to "love the Lord your God with all your heart and with all your soul and with all your mind and with all your strength" (Mark 12:30). To come to the text with a cold and skeptical attitude is to come to Jesus with disinterest.

Yet we can only come to the Bible as we are, with our mistaken beliefs, our constant struggles, our joyful praises and our heartrending doubts. When we engage the Bible with our whole life, we're reading it with spiritual passion, an approach Paul ardently proclaimed.

> The Spirit searches all things, even the deep things of God. For who among men knows the thoughts of a man except the man's spirit within him? In the same way, no one knows the thoughts of God except the Spirit of God. We have not received the spirit of the world but the Spirit who is from God, that we may understand what God has freely given us. This is what we speak, not in words taught us by human wisdom but in words taught by the Spirit, expressing spiritual truths in spiritual words. The man without the Spirit does not accept the things that come from the Spirit of God, for they are foolishness to him, and he cannot understand them because they are spiritually discerned. The spiritual man makes judgments about all things, but he himself is not subject to any man's judgment:
>
> "For who has known the mind of the Lord
>   that he may instruct him?"
> But we have the mind of Christ. (1 Corinthians 2:10-16)

Paul argues here that he is speaking words the Spirit told him to speak. People who do not know the Spirit will not understand Paul's message, but those in whom the Spirit lives will be able to recognize that God is speaking through him. This passage is the starting point for all Bible reading, telling us that we must read the Bible with a passion fueled by the Spirit. Why? Because it is the Holy Spirit who connects us with the Bible. When we become Christians, the Spirit takes up residence within us to help us understand His words in the Word. We begin speaking the same language as the Bible.

Our attitude, then, should have the same vitality as that expressed by the wise teacher of Proverbs 2:1-6.[1]

> My son, if you accept my words
>   and store up my commands within you,
> turning your ear to wisdom
>   and applying your heart to understanding,
> and if you call out for insight
>   and cry aloud for understanding,
> and if you look for it as for silver
>   and search for it as for hidden treasure,
> then you will understand the fear of the LORD
>   and find the knowledge of God.
> For the LORD gives wisdom,
>   and from his mouth come knowledge and
>   understanding.

This passage describes no dispassionate, scientific scrutiny of the text but rather a wholehearted, even desperate desire to know the teaching of the Father. For us, the object of the search for knowledge is not a thing, not just a book or any other impersonal object. It is God Himself.

Such passion isn't reserved for the biblical writers alone. It is for all of us because all of us yearn for the work of God in our lives, even if it thrusts us into tough new challenges. For the intimate knowledge of God is the only thing worthy of our lifelong search. It's a priceless relationship worthy of the deepest passion. Listen to poet John Donne as he pours out his desire for God:

> Batter my heart, three-personed God; for, you
> As yet but knock, breathe, shine, and seek to mend;
> That I may rise, and stand, o'erthrow me, and bend
> Your force, to break, blow, burn, and make me new . . .

Divorce me, untie, or break that knot again,
Take me to you, imprison me, for I
Except you enthrall me, never shall be free,
Nor ever chaste, except you ravish me.[2]

Have you ever wanted the reality of God so desperately?

He is waiting for you—in the Word. But how will you see Him there?

GRINDING THE SPIRITUAL LENSES

We have already spoken of Bible reading by using the metaphor of lenses. So let's continue that analogy in order to be very practical about how we can approach the Bible with deep spiritual passion. Bruce Waltke cites Martin Luther in suggesting that we can take up certain disciplines that will "grind our spiritual lenses" in preparation for reading the Word of God.[3] These spiritual exercises have to do with prayer, contemplation, and personal experience.

The dialogue of prayer. Prayer is the beginning of a dialogue with God, whom we meet in the pages of Scripture. It puts us in an attitude of worship. Through prayer, we acknowledge that we are entering holy ground. We are in the presence of God as we read.

As we pray, we can bring our cares and concerns to our heavenly Father, asking Him to build us up, to encourage us in the midst of suffering. We can look for an affirmation of forgiveness when we're grappling with guilt. We can read the Bible to find guidance in our daily life as we struggle to follow God in a world that wants to tear us away from Him.

Prayer is so much more than just the words we speak as we fold our hands for a few moments before opening the Bible or the words of thanks we utter after we are through reading. Prayer is an attitude of openness and submission to our Lord Jesus Christ, into whose presence we enter as we read. It is an opening of our hearts to Him, even if we have no words at all. As Thomas Brooks once said: "God hears no more than the heart speaks; and if the heart be dumb, God will certainly be deaf."

It's true, we can close ourselves off to God by closing off the supposedly secret parts of our lives, the parts that may be hurting the most. But He is already in those parts too, waiting for us to acknowledge Him there, awaiting our permission to apply His healing, transforming power. Thus, in prayer, we subject ourselves to the critique of the Word rather than the other way around.

The quietness of contemplation. Modern life moves at a hectic pace. Have you noticed? Few escape the wildness of the world at the turning of the millennium. Technological advances throughout the twentieth century have promised more and more leisure but have mostly succeeded in accelerating the pace of our lives. For example, the automobile cut down on the time it takes to get from one place to another, but because of our cars we go more places. More recently, the development of personal computers has cut down the time it takes to produce a written document. Instead of leading to more time for reflection, however, our computers simply generate more documents to wade through. And the Internet makes it easier than ever to communicate across the world through writing. But now, instead of getting a couple of letters a day from the post office, I find dozens of e-mail messages awaiting me each evening!

We rush here and there, *doing* so much — without much time to think, or just to *be*. It appears that our attention spans have atrophied. Technologies have increased some of our abilities and decreased others. When the printing press was introduced, books could be mass-produced and reach more people, but the power of the memory eroded. We don't know yet how the new cyber-technologies will affect our abilities, but they will surely have some negative affects. No doubt the recent technological developments will only increase the hectic pace of our lives, further damaging the possibility for reflection.

Of course, the point isn't to reject the advances and throw away our computers, sell our televisions, and start riding bicycles down the interstate. Rather, we need to take steps to exercise the spiritual discipline of reflection in the midst of our fast-paced world.

My own daily routine is a testimony to the frantic pace of life and my failure to make room for contemplation, for just being in God's presence. I rush from class to do research on my next book. At the last possible moment I jump into my car to attend my son's soccer game. I hurry home for supper, often have a meeting later that evening, and then return breathless to wish my wife and three boys goodnight. On weekends I either do chores or head off on a trip to speak in a church or school. With all this rushing *toward* things, what am I *avoiding*?

Have you ever asked yourself the same question? I've found that, in the midst of all my busyness, an intense loneliness calls to me. It is no doubt a blessed calling from the Lord — to slow down, to "be still, and know that I am God" (see Psalm 46:10). Henri Nouwen, in his book *The Wounded Healer*, put it this way:

> The Christian way of life does not take away our loneliness; it protects and cherishes it as a precious gift. Sometimes it seems as if we do everything possible to avoid the painful confrontation with our basic human loneliness, and allow ourselves to be trapped by false gods promising immediate satisfaction and quick relief. Our loneliness reveals to us an inner emptiness that can be destructive when misunderstood, but filled with promise for him who can tolerate its sweet pain.[4]

I invite you to make time for this sweet pain while coming to the Word of God. When? For me, the best time for reflection is on an airplane! I have to fight for time to contemplate. When is it best for you? When can you make some time to focus on what's happening inside and to bring it all before God with inner quietness?

With such quietness of heart and mind, we can come to the Word for profitable reading. The Bible is both a simple and a complex book. It may be easily understood on one level, but it takes a lifetime just to scratch the surface of its richness.

The Bible is a book to savor and think about. It is also a long book, so it may be necessary to read large tracts of it at a fairly rapid rate in order to get a feel for the whole. But it is also a book of depth requiring quiet and prayerful reflection. With this in mind, why not employ a two-track reading strategy? On the one hand, read three or four chapters a day in order to get through the Bible within a year's time. But then choose a book or a section of a book for special study and read just a few verses. Then spend ten minutes, not reading, but asking how the passage reveals Christ to you and how the passage can be incarnated in your life. Prayer combined with such contemplation leads to an open heart in God's presence.

The saturation of personal experience. The Bible needs to permeate our entire lives. Just as we should pray without ceasing (see 1 Thessalonians 5:17), we ought to read the Bible without ceasing. But how can we do this? Should we seek only solitude and avoid worldly activities, like the hermit monks of old?

When Paul told Christians to pray continually, he didn't mean to constantly be in *conscious* dialogue with God. Rather, he intended Christians to develop an ever ready openness to hear God no matter what they were doing. So, too, the Bible should be such a rich part of our lives — thoroughly saturating our personal experience — that, though we may not have a Bible with us, its message is constantly before our minds and in our hearts wherever we are.

Thomas Carlyle, the nineteenth-century Scottish historian, said, "Our grand business is not to see what lies dimly at a distance, but to do what lies clearly at hand." As we let the words of Scripture permeate our lives, our interpretation will become quite practical and lead to loving good works within our daily routines. We'll escape the arid, profitless arena of mere academic study. The Word will, like the seed, grow in the rich soil of our hearts, becoming a part of us, helping us to grow as human beings, compelling us to become more like Christ.

IMITATING THE LORD

Becoming like Jesus is the goal of our existence, and the simple truth is that Jesus studied the Bible. He knew the Bible. He often settled controversies with His religious opponents by appealing to the Bible (see Matthew 22:29). His life was guided by the Bible (John 13:18). He shared the great teachings of the Bible concerning Himself with His disciples (Luke 24:32). He expected all of God's people to be diligent students of the Bible, so much so that when they displayed insufficient biblical understanding, He reprimanded them harshly: "Haven't you read this scripture?" (Mark 12:10).

We are called to imitate Christ, and His own actions stir us to follow Him. If we desire to be like Him, we will become diligent students of the Bible. But let's take this further: if we desire to be like Christ and are growing to be like Him, we must practice being intimate with Him on a daily basis. Yet the analogy typically used to describe wise Bible readers is the scientist. According to this model, the Bible is our object of study, and we approach it as a blank slate in order to avoid reading into it our own ideas, seeing only what we want to see. So the "science" of interpretation becomes formulaic, consisting of rules by which we can read the Bible with integrity.

Much that is important needs to be retained from this model (and we draw upon it in this book), but it is distorted. For one thing, it leads us into thinking that we can be objective, when in fact we are not since we can never really divest ourselves of who we are as we approach the Bible. Second, it makes our relationship to the Bible into a relationship between a person and an object. Indeed, the physical *book* that we read — ink on paper in a binding — is an object, but the *relationship* is between two persons. God, after all, speaks to us through the voices of many human authors.

Are you willing to think of your relationship with the Bible as part of a conversation with a Person? Think of your own best friendships and ask yourself how long they would last if you studied them rather than loved them. Carrying the analogy further, think about what happens when you "tune out" in conversation with a friend. You do all the talking but don't listen to what your friend has to say. Obviously, the relationship can suffer harm when such neglect becomes characteristic. But when, out of love and interest, we listen intently to what our friend says, we learn more and more about him or her. Since it is all about our developing intimate relationship, the Bible should keep us on the edge of our seats as we listen to the Person who is most important to us. We don't want to fall into the trap of studying God; we want to fall in love with Him.

Can we find a better model, then, than a scientist to describe the wise Bible reader?

How about an artist? Artists are passionate people. They don't study the world with their minds only but with their whole beings. They lean toward intuition rather than strict logic in their thinking. They aren't ruled by an unbending method of study, but they do follow their instincts and experience. Much of this book will offer methods for studying the Bible and suggest right ways and warn about wrong ways to read it. However, these methods and suggestions should be taken as principles rather than rules. They should be applied as art rather than science. In this way, the Bible becomes more and more awe-inspiring for us, a masterwork of art from the Creator's hand. What else could do a better job of stirring our passion for Him?

I am reminded of a little story that makes this point about spiritual passion—a point that our friend Ralph at the beginning of this chapter clearly needed to embrace. It seems that a pastor became bored and said to another pastor, "I'm tired of this routine existence. Let's do something extraordinary, startling, magnificent; something that will make our brains whirl and our hearts leap."

"Okay," replied the other.

And so, after a moment of meaningful silence, they both went back to their studies to read the Word.

PART III

The Understanding Mind

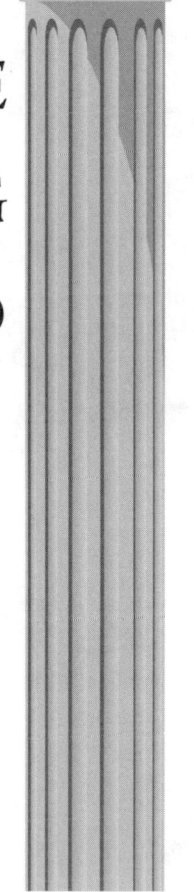

6

IS THE BIBLE TRUSTWORTHY?

"I thought there was nothing new under the sun!"

The comment rang out in the locker room as I rested briefly after my routine thirty minutes on the stair climbing machine. John, a man I often saw around the gym, had been examining something lying on a table — a strange object that no one could identify.

"Ecclesiastes," I said. "You just quoted the book of Ecclesiastes."

We introduced ourselves and, upon discovering that I was a professor of Old Testament studies, John uttered another loud comment: "You shouldn't have told me that. I have a lot of trouble with the Bible, and I don't mind telling you about it."

"Fire away," I said.

"Okay. Maybe the Bible is divinely inspired, but

even if I grant you that, what we have is the product of human effort and thought. After all, we don't have the original writings; we have later copies. Furthermore, we don't read the original Hebrew and Greek; we read translations. And these translations are made by fallible humans, so they have given us fallible texts. How can I entrust my life to a bunch of human documents, even if their origins are divine?"

SOME GOOD QUESTIONS

I have to admit, John raised some excellent points. Have you, too, ever wondered about these things? Does what we have before us really represent God's Word to His people? Or is this Book a strange, unidentifiable object, irreparably marred by human error and weakness?

I had only five minutes to respond to John because I had to catch a plane. What astounded me was that by the end of that five minutes everyone in the gym had gathered around to listen. Though not religious people, they were vitally interested in hearing something about where the Bible came from and whether its present form communicated or betrayed its supposed divine origins.

The Bible we have in our hands has come a long way, so it's natural for us to raise questions about its present integrity. These writings began in the hoary past when prophets and apostles claimed to bring their contemporaries a divine message. Is that what actually happened? If so, then we can assume that the message was intended by God for more than the immediate audience and that He therefore providentially guided its transmission down through the ages. But let's explore the foundations for such assumptions by looking more closely at how the Bible actually came into being. We'll consider five critical issues related to the Bible's development — things I might have covered with John if I had had the time: its composition, canonicity, transmission, translations, and incarnational nature.

COMPOSITION: WHO WROTE IT?

Who authored the Bible? When and how was it written? Did the authors know that God was moving them to write sacred Scripture? These are valid questions that occasionally cross the minds of thoughtful readers.

When we stop to think about it, the answers to these questions, as far as we know them, are quite surprising. God used many people, from many different walks of life, to bring His Word into existence. Kings, prophets, farmers, priests, eccentrics, perhaps a doctor, scholars—all were called upon by God to bring His written Word to humanity.

The first written Scripture comes from the time of Moses, which I date to the fifteenth century B.C.[1] The latest writing is perhaps the book of Revelation, which is dated by many to the end of the first century, A.D. The rest of Scripture comes from the time period between these dates.[2] It is interesting to note, however, that the outflowing of Scripture falls within four distinct periods of history: the time of Moses, the rule of David and Solomon, the time surrounding the exile to Babylon, and the time right after Jesus' death and resurrection. The only truly silent period is the so-called intertestamental period, from about 400 B.C. to the beginning of the New Testament epistles in the first century A.D.

Did the Bible's writers feel the inspiration of God within them? Certainly many of the prophets sensed God's guiding hand as they spoke in His name, and they didn't hesitate to identify their words with the words of the Lord of the universe. But we cannot be sure they all were conscious of the great significance of their work. We do know that God never overrode their individual personalities, as we can see by noting their varied styles of writing. Luke, for instance, wrote in an educated Greek. Compare that to fisherman John's simpler language and more limited vocabulary.

We tend to think that when a prophet or apostle wrote Scripture that he sat down for a period of time and concentrated on his work, from beginning to end, until it was finished. That is how we would write a letter or report today. Actually, the evidence shows that different biblical books came into existence in different ways. Sometimes a prophet did sit down and write his prophecy in one sitting. At other times, a Bible book (such as Jeremiah) was the product of a long ministry and came into existence in various stages. Still other writers drew upon available sources (from a king's historical records, for instance), and sometimes biblical books were added to by other inspired prophets before the period of inspiration ended. You can learn more about how a specific writer approached his work by consulting a good introduction or commentary related to each specific Bible book.

CANON: WHY THESE BOOKS?

The term canon means "standard" or "rule." With regard to the Bible, the canon refers to the sacred writings that God's people use as their standard of faith and practice. They are the writings upon which believers base their lives. But why these writings and no others? What is so special about them?

As Christians living at the turn of the second millennium, we don't often reflect on the canonical status of the Bible; we simply accept it. Our Bible is something that is "given" to us as a completed whole. We grow up with the idea that the sixty-six books of the Bible are fixed, and we aren't actively debating whether some new book ought to be added or another removed. We just accept what is there, though we might wonder why in the world God wanted a certain book, like the Song of Songs, in His Word.

Then again, we might have a Roman Catholic friend. Borrowing her Bible, we open it up and see some strange titles: The Wisdom of Solomon, Tobit, Baruch, and The Song of the Three. Where did these books, commonly called the Apocrypha, come from? And why do Catholic believers read these books and Protestants not include them in their Bibles? This kind of inquiry might lead to the broader question of why we accept *any* books at all as God-given. What makes a book canonical?

The key thing to remember about the canon is that human beings have not invested these books with their authority; they are inherently authoritative. They do not become canonical once we accept them as such, but they are authoritative by virtue of the fact that God is their ultimate author. They speak with the voice of God, and we are to accept them as such. In other words, the church does not define the canon; the canon defines the church.

There were, however, in the early days of the church, canonical councils organized for the purpose of surveying the writings that believers were using in their worship and devotional lives. The councils simply *recognized* those writings as having proven their God-given authority. By the year 400 A.D., the canon—the list of Scripture books as we now have it—was likely complete. Christians through the centuries have widely agreed on these books, though Catholics and Protestants differ in their view of how much authority resides in the Apocryphal writings. (For Protestants, the Apocryphal books provide good devotional reading, just as any book from the local Christian bookstore might be helpful today.)

Perhaps putting our faith in the Bible is made harder by the fact that the canonical books do not have an obvious trait that makes them different from all other ancient writings. Yes, some of them claim divine inspiration pretty clearly. The prophets of the Old Testament constantly call out "Thus says the Lord" and claim to speak in the name of God. But most of the books do not speak that directly, and we have writings from the same historical periods that do claim direct inspiration but are not in our Bible.

Surprisingly, not even divine revelation is the sole criterion of canonicity. For God has revealed more than is canonical. Before Moses wrote, the people of God knew and spoke with God, but these revelations are not part of our Bible. Paul wrote other letters that we do not have (Colossians 4:16 refers to a letter to the Laodiceans), and even if we discover them they would not become a part of our Bible. The Bible, then, is not *just* God's revelation. It is the part of revelation that is *intended to be the standard of faith and practice* for God's people through the ages.

Our discussion so far is, of course, sort of circular, for we are asking how we know that the Bible is God's Word. Our answer is to say that its authenticity was self-evident from the beginning. Does that sound like an overly daring leap of faith? If so, remember that such a "leap" is something we have to do in almost every area of human inquiry. As Christian apologist C. S. Lewis once said: "If nothing is self-evident, then nothing can be proved." It's true, isn't it? All of our most basic principles, especially in philosophy and religion, must start with unprovable assumptions about the nature of reality that must either be accepted by all — or no further discussion can follow. One such assumption is, "It is true that when I am thinking, I am doing something that is rational." Now that statement can't be proven from some outside source. But everyone accepts it, by faith, as self-evident. Otherwise, attempting a conversation would be silly. What would be the point?

Additionally, if our belief in God and the Bible were based purely and primarily on logic and deductive evidence, then only the smartest people would be Christians. But Paul tells us that belief is not based on the intellect but on faith, which is a gift from God. The passage from 1 Corinthians 2 that I quoted in the last chapter is relevant here again: "The man without the Spirit does not accept the things that come from the Spirit of God, for they are foolishness to him, and he cannot understand them, because they are spiritually discerned" (verse 14). Paul goes on to argue that the spiritual person (that is, the one who possesses the Spirit of God) can make such judgments because "we have the mind of Christ" (verse 16). Ultimately, it is the Holy Spirit who convinces us of these important truths (see 1 Thessalonians 1:5).

Nonetheless, while our belief concerning the Bible as canon is a matter of faith, we can find some relief in the strong evidence that the

Bible we accept as divinely given is the right one. This is not the place to lay out all the evidence because there is so much. At this point, though, I want to point out that we accept the same Bible as did our Lord Jesus Christ. Roger Beckwith, in a powerful study of the early rabbinic sources, has shown that there is no doubt that the Pharisees of the first century A.D. had a Bible that was exactly like the Old Testament we read today.[3] And when Jesus got into debates with these religious leaders, He appealed to Scripture to silence them (see Mark 12:28-40 for an example). There was no debate about the standard, or rule, that governed their arguments; they both appealed to the same authority. In other words, though many deep issues separated Jesus and the Pharisees, they were united in their understanding of what constituted the Word of God. Thus when Christians accept the Old Testament without the Apocrypha as the Word of God, they are following in the practice of their Lord and Savior Jesus Christ.

But what about the New Testament? No part of the New Testament was written until after Jesus' death and resurrection. He did not affirm them, so how do we know that these books are divinely inspired? We might begin a response by first recognizing the need for a written record and interpretation of the great acts of Jesus' earthly ministry. Once the eyewitnesses were gone, something was needed to let the future generations know what had happened and to explain the significance of these great redemptive events. Who better to do that than the apostles? Passages like Ephesians 2:19-20 show the importance of the apostles to the establishment of the church.

> You are fellow citizens with God's people and members of
> God's household, built on the foundation of the apostles and
> prophets, with Christ Jesus himself as the chief cornerstone.

The prophets, who predicted the ministry of Jesus, gave us the Old Testament. Then Jesus, through His death and resurrection, brought the church into existence. The apostles of the church experienced the climax of God's great plan of redemption with their eyewitness testimony, and they left a written record for later generations. The revelation of the prophets, of Jesus, of the apostles makes a progressive whole. Notice how Peter equated the words of the prophets and the apostles in his second letter: "I want you to recall the words spoken in the past by the holy prophets and the command given by our Lord and Savior through your apostles" (2 Peter 3:2). A little later he specifically equated Paul's writings with Scripture (see 3:14-16). So, once again, we will be a bit circular and say that the New Testament itself witnesses to its own authority and that this is confirmed by the smooth progress of revelation and the belief and practice of the church down through the ages.

Ultimately, though, our belief in the authority of both Testaments rests with our decision about the resurrection of Christ. This is the call to faith that confronts everyone who hears the gospel message: Did Jesus truly rise from the dead? After checking all the evidence, if we answer yes, then we are dealing with the most unusual Person ever to enter human history. Here is a Person who claimed to be God and then proved it by leaving behind an empty tomb—and countless followers who were willing to die for Him! Yes, if He is the risen Lord, then we can be confident that everything He ever said was the truth. This applies to His words about Scripture, as well.

Regarding the Old Testament: "I tell you the truth, until heaven and earth disappear, not the smallest letter, not the least stroke of a pen, will by any means disappear from the Law until everything is accomplished." (Matthew 5:18)

Regarding the New Testament: "But when he, the Spirit of truth, comes, he will guide you into all truth. He will not speak on his own; he will speak only what he hears, and he will tell you what is yet to come." (John 16:13)

TRANSMISSION: IS IT ACCURATE?

Some people are unnecessarily disturbed by the fact that we do not have a single piece of the Bible's original parchment and ink. The technical name for the first written form of a biblical text is *autograph.* The Hebrews and Greeks wrote mostly on perishable materials like leather and papyrus. Only rarely are such written materials preserved through the ages. (A well-known example is the Dead Sea Scrolls, which were found in caves in an extremely dry climate on the northwest corner of the Dead Sea area.) Since hundreds, even thousands of years separate the original writings from our contemporary translations, many people assume that the text is riddled with errors that have arisen due to careless scribes.

Since we don't have those original pieces of leather or papyrus, it remains for biblical scholars to compare the copied portions that have survived and then compile a single biblical text from them. Does that make sense to you? It would be as if you had written a letter to your mother and then she made photocopies to send to all your relatives. But suppose your mother then lost the original letter. No problem! There would still be dozens of copies around for anyone to discover what you had written. Of course, if your mother had made the copies by handwriting each one rather than by photocopying, then some of the copies might be slightly different from others. A comma might be missing in this one, a word added or left out of that one. By comparing all the copies, though, a person could reassemble the words of the original with great confidence.

That is what scholars do with thousands of copies of the original autographs, in a literary science called textual criticism. They compare the copies that come from various dates in ancient times and use them to assemble a complete Hebrew and Greek text that reflects the errorless original. They also make notes about any textual "variants" (those minor differences in spelling and wording, similar to what would have occurred in Mom's hand-copied letters to your relatives).

In light of the little variations in the copies, we have to say that no single ancient Hebrew or Greek manuscript portion preserves an ideal, error-free text. We have many manuscripts and versions of the Bible going back hundreds of years, and they do show variations as they are compared with one another. But the truly amazing thing is how similar they are and how minor the differences. With this in mind, a couple of observations should set you at ease about whether you are reading God's Word or the results of human ineptitude.[4]

First, remember that modern translations are based on an extremely reliable textual base. One reason we know this is because of an amazing discovery back in the 1940s: the Dead Sea Scrolls. Here's what I mean. Hebrew scholars work primarily from the oldest complete manuscript of the Old Testament (called Codex Leningradensis), which dates from A.D. 1006. To be sure, this is more than a millennium after the last Old Testament book was written. Yet when we compare it with the earlier manuscript portions, especially the Dead Sea Scrolls (which provide texts from about 150 B.C. to A.D. 100), and the Septuagint (a Greek translation, which in some instances takes us a century earlier than that), we find astounding similarity in the readings. Over a period of a thousand years the text was faithfully and accurately copied by hand. Such comparisons prove it.

The New Testament manuscript fragments do have many more variants among them than the Old Testament portions. But that is partly because we have many more copies of the original autographs, and earlier ones at that. Early papyri, uncials (manuscripts in all capital letters), miniscules (manuscripts in all lowercase letters), and lectionaries, as well as citations in the writings of early church fathers, provide numerous witnesses to the original text. And keep in mind that the vast majority of the variants are merely differences in spelling or grammar that are of no significance to the meaning of the text.

The bottom line of our first observation is that the evidence overwhelmingly supports an astoundingly accurate transmission of the Bible. Our Hebrew and Greek texts are extremely close to the original writings of the prophets and apostles. Through the exercise of textual criticism, we know that we have arrived at a highly reliable Bible.

This observation leads to a second one: In no case does textual transmission blur our understanding of any significant teaching of the Bible. Sure, there are some important textual issues that we wish we could resolve with perfect certainty, but no fundamental doctrine is affected by lack of certainty about the text. To question Christianity because we don't have the original autographs is simply to raise a nonexistent problem in order to avoid dealing with the claims of Christ.

TRANSLATIONS: WHY SO MANY?

Few Christians can read Hebrew and Greek, the two major languages of the Bible. And fewer still can read Aramaic, the language used in parts of Ezra and Daniel. Therefore, translation plays a key role in our access to God's Word.

English-speaking Christians have an unprecedented richness in their translation options. Instead of moaning, "Not another translation," when a new version appears, we should get on our knees and thank God for His gifts to this part of the church! And we can throw our support behind the efforts to translate God's Word into other languages, as well.

The point is that multiple translations serve two important purposes. First, they meet the differing needs of various kinds of people. Children, or people who speak English as a second language, and adults with limited reading skills benefit greatly from translations that utilize a simple vocabulary and sentence structure (for example: *The New Century Version,* also called *The Everyday Bible*). Readers who have a high level of literary sophistication might gravitate toward *The King James Version* or *The New Revised Standard Version.* Others, who want a relatively bland, but literal text will use *The New International Version.* Still others, who like the combination of exegetical accuracy with a vibrant and interesting English style, will like *The New Living Translation. The New American Standard Bible* rightly has the reputation as the most literal translation around. It is a highly regarded study Bible, but many people do not prefer it for devotional reading. Many people use several translations, depending on their primary purpose during any particular reading—literal translations for studying words and syntax, looser paraphrases for focusing on the overall flow of ideas in contemporary idiom.

The second purpose of multiple translations is to enable us to get a better picture of the original language because no language can be exactly translated to another. Language is fluid and full of nuances; words have a "feel" as well as meaning. To be sure, any one of the versions I've mentioned is accurate and reliable. But you will get a richer understanding of the original text when you read from more than one. I suggest starting with a translation whose concern it is to communicate the message of the original text to modern readers like ourselves. In my opinion, no version does that better than the *New Living Translation*. The *New International Version* is a close second but tends to be a bit more wooden and difficult for a modern reader to understand. Then use two more Bibles: a more literal text, and a freer paraphrasing text. The first gives you a feel for the original text, though it does not communicate the message as well to English speakers. For this purpose I recommend *The New International Version, The New American Standard Version,* or *The New Revised Standard Version.* Then, the most interesting paraphrase available is being written by Eugene Peterson. His New Testament, *The Message,* is available now, and he is presently translating the Old Testament, and it is available in parts.

INCARNATION: HOW DO WE BRIDGE THE DISTANCE?

The Bible is the Word of God incarnate. From our review of the process that brought us the Bible, we see that it did not simply drop out of heaven. The analogy, of course, is with Jesus. Jesus was fully God and fully human. Yet He did not just drop out of heaven but came into the world through the process of gestation and birth—a remarkable conception to be sure but a birth process nonetheless. He was a particular human being, a Jewish male who lived in the first century A.D.. He was a human but without sin.

As the Word of God incarnate, the Bible's ultimate origin is also divine; its more immediate source is human. It came into existence by the type of literary "birth processes" typical of any human composition. Human beings took up writing instruments and wrote symbols on a page. The books of the Bible are particular writings, written in a specific known language, using genres and other writing conventions common in the secular writings of the day. The result was a collection of writings developed over sixty generations, written by scores of people on three different continents, covering hundreds of controversial subjects with harmony and absolute continuity from Genesis through Revelation. This astounding unity makes the written Word a truly miraculous incarnation.

And the incarnational aspect of the Bible means that God spoke to His people in a way that they understood. He used Hebrew, not some new divine language. As we will see later in this book, God used typical ancient Near Eastern literary forms like history, law, wisdom, prophetic writings, as well as Palestinian-Hellenistic forms like the epistle. This simple fact means that *there is a distance between us and the original audience* that needs to be bridged for proper understanding to take place. Yes, we are somewhat separated from the Bible by virtue of the language, culture, and literary conventions of its first readers.

How shall we bridge that distance? The rest of this book is devoted to exploring the ways in which we can go back to the text and build a solid applicational bridge into our lives today, for our primary purpose is to read the Bible so it reads us like a mirror, transforms us like a seed, and reveals Jesus Christ to us as a close friend, here and now.

> After all, it is personal experience that counts. And if anyone has reason to doubt the inspiration of the Bible, the certain yet simple test to apply is to yield oneself to its power, strive faithfully to follow its commands, act as it suggests. As a result, the conviction will irresistibly grow upon the mind seeking proof in this way, that its claim to be inspired of God is not to be questioned, but reverently received as just and undeniable.[5]

In other words: Take up and read with a fully engaged heart and mind!

7
WHAT'S THE MEANING HERE?

In a recent comedy, the lead character approached the woman of his dreams and asked, "Mary, what do you think are the chances of a girl like you and a guy like me getting together?"

"Well, John, I would have to say about one in a million."

With that, John breaks out in a huge smile. With a sigh of great relief, he exclaims, "So . . . you're saying there's a chance!"

GETTING IT RIGHT

John interpreted Mary's words—and got them all wrong. Has it ever happened to you?

It's no exaggeration to say we're constantly interpreting. As we launch into our day we interpret our moods, our conversations, the morning newspaper, the traffic signs, the look on our boss's face. Some of these acts of interpretation are so natural and frequent that we don't give them a thought. As I drove to work this morning and saw the light over the intersection turn red, I stopped without weighing the pros and cons.

In other cases, interpretation takes work. In conversation we often ask others for clarification and elaboration so we can really understand what they're trying to communicate to us. We want to understand exactly what they intend to tell us (unless, like John, we're more interested in hearing what we want to hear).

Books and other forms of writing are even more difficult to interpret. We're engaged in a conversation with the author, but the author isn't there to respond when we seek clarification. We don't have the luxury of asking Shakespeare what he was talking about in a particularly obscure section of *Hamlet*.

Similarly, the Bible demands our full interpretive energies if we are to get the meaning just right. After all, the Bible puts us in a rather unique conversation. First, it thrusts us into dialogue with a wide variety of human authors, from Moses, who lived around 1500 B.C., to John, the author of the book of Revelation, who lived at the end of the first century A.D. Most important, the Bible puts us into conversation with our God. For these reasons we need accurate interpretation—an understanding of Scripture that coincides with God's intention.

This raises a problem, however. The Bible isn't always easy to understand. Take a quick look at the episode recorded in Exodus 4:24-26, for example. A Bible version such as *The New International Version* supplies names that aren't in the Hebrew text to make the action more clear. But not even the most experienced Hebrew scholar is confident about what Zipporah is doing or whose foreskin she's throwing at whose feet.

Even when the text seems straightforward, we may feel uncertain about our interpretation of it. The words in Ecclesiastes 7:16-18 are easy enough to read and understand:

> Do not be overrighteous,
>   neither be overwise—
>   why destroy yourself?
> Do not be overwicked,
>   and do not be a fool—
>   why die before your time?

It is good to grasp the one
    and not let go of the other.

But can the Teacher really mean that we should not be too wicked or too righteous? Is he really advocating the golden mean — that a little bit of wickedness is good for the soul?

Even when we do understand a passage correctly, we may fail to see its place in the rest of the Bible and distort its application. For instance, we may read the speeches of Job's three friends and make the fatal mistake of applying them as normative biblical teaching. When Zophar stated in Job 20:5, "the mirth of the wicked is brief, the joy of the godless lasts but a moment," we might wrongly wonder why our godless neighbor has enjoyed material prosperity and happiness for as long as we've known him.

All of us want to treat the Word of God with the respect it deserves, and we certainly don't want to read into it things that aren't there. For these reasons, we need to apply the basic principles of hermeneutics — the science of interpretation — as we read the Bible. These principles aren't laws set in stone, and they should never be applied mechanically as a kind of academic exercise. But used wisely, they can help anyone get a better grasp on the intended meaning of Scripture. Here they are:

Principle 1: Look for the author's intended meaning. Each biblical passage has an objective meaning intended by its author. The interpreter's task is to discover that meaning. This principle seems clear enough, but we must come to grips with a couple of issues it raises.

First, who is the author and how do we uncover his intention? Even when we know the name of the human author (Moses, Paul, David), we have no independent access to him. We can't ask Paul whether he referred to Christians or nonChristians when he described a person who doesn't do what God wants in Romans 7:21-25. We can only answer such questions by placing ourselves in the time period when the author wrote and ask what he meant to tell us.

A second issue has to do with the unique character of the Bible as the Word of God. As 2 Peter 1:21 states, "Prophecy never had its origin in the will of man, but men spoke from God as they were carried along by the Holy Spirit." God is the ultimate author of the Bible, and this important truth has implications for how we understand it. Let's look at an example in Hosea 11:1:

When Israel was a child, I loved him,
and out of Egypt I called my son.

Who is the author of this passage? According to the first verse of Hosea, it's the prophet by that name. But how can we know his intention in the words of this passage? First, we know approximately when Hosea lived. We also have the broader context of the whole book, which gives us a more complete idea of what Hosea intended to say in this one verse. When we study this text in the context of his entire book, we find that Hosea is referring to the Exodus described in the book of Exodus.

Later we may be reading Matthew 2 and come across verse 15. Here the writer applies Hosea 11:1 to Jesus as a youth returning to Judea from Egypt. This reference doesn't seem in keeping with Hosea's intention. Yet here we must remember where the meaning of a text finally resides — in the intention of God, its ultimate author. As we read this passage in the context of the whole Bible, we see that God has made an analogy. He is prophetically relating Israel (God's children, being freed from Egypt) to Jesus (God's Child, coming up from Egypt). This is a pattern that runs throughout Matthew's gospel.

Notice that this principle acknowledges there *is* a meaning to the text. That's an important point in our age of relativism. A number of scholarly interpreters of the Bible, mostly university professors, suggest that the Bible has no set meaning and that we may read into it whatever we want. On the contrary, when we interpret the Bible we are looking for the author's original meaning, not imposing our own meaning. When the reader's interpretation conflicts with the author's intention, the reader's interpretation is wrong.

Principle 2: Read the passage in context. With the Bible, as with all good literature, we must get a grasp of the whole in order to appreciate and understand the parts. We ought never treat a biblical book as a collection of isolated passages. They are connected stories, poems, and letters. The meaning of the individual verses can only be discovered in the flow of the whole literary piece.

This principle does not stop us from turning to the middle of a biblical book and reading a section, but we should only do so if we have a basic understanding of how the passage fits into the message of the whole book. In other words, when we read little bits and pieces of Scripture, we should exercise great caution. Otherwise, we might distort God's message.

As a new Christian wanting to obey God, a college friend of mine one day searched through Scripture for guidance about getting married. His eyes fell on 1 Corinthians 7:27, "Are you unmarried? Do not look for a wife." At first this confused him, and, having grown up in a church tradition that prized a celibate priesthood, it didn't seem too far off the mark to him. But as he read in the context of the whole book, he saw, much to his relief, that Paul did not forbid Christians to marry.

The context includes more than just the paragraphs before and after a text. It is an ever-expanding thematic backdrop. For example, consider Genesis 50:20, where Joseph said, "You intended to harm me, but God intended it for good to accomplish . . . the saving of many lives." If we look at the immediate context, we will see that he is speaking to his brothers right after his father had died. To understand what he's referring to we need to read the entire Joseph story in Genesis 37:1–50:26. Then we see that Joseph's brothers sold him to Midianite traders who took him to Egypt. We also observe how God used their evil actions to put Joseph in a position of power, which eventually allowed him to save his family.

But there's an even broader context to consider. If we read Genesis 50:20 in light of the whole book of Genesis, we bring in the promise that God gave to Abraham—about numerous descendants and land. No doubt Joseph reflects on the past, and his statement shows his awareness that God had overruled his brothers' evil intentions in order to preserve the family line and fulfill God's promise to Abraham.

We're still not done with the context, however. The ultimate context of any particular passage is the whole Bible. As we read the Bible we see many parallels to Joseph's statement but none so vivid as the words of Peter when he described Jesus' death. In Acts 2:22-24 Peter says that Jesus was killed by men who had evil intentions, but God used those very intentions to save many from their sin.

We can learn to read in context by reading whole books of the Bible rather than just little snippets. If you can sit down for two or three hours to read a novel, try doing the same with Isaiah or Acts, but make sure you do it with a contemporary English version. Whenever you do read a short passage, read it with an outline of the whole book in mind or with the help of a good commentary.

The exact nature of the context may differ from book to book. The context of the historical books comes from the flow of events in the story. In the epistles, or letters, one idea builds upon another. In Proverbs, chapters 10 through 31 have a looser context. In these chapters, one pithy proverb—on laziness, for example—is followed by two on the tongue and then another on laziness. Still, in all biblical books we should have a sense of the whole book as we study any part of it. Always ask yourself how a passage fits into the message of the whole book, even the whole Bible.

Principle 3: Identify the genre of the passage. Written texts come in a variety of forms. A genre of literature is a group of texts that share similarity in content, tone, or structure. We're familiar with genre in a library or a bookstore. Books are either fiction or nonfiction. Fiction can be divided into novels, mystery, romance, science fiction, and so on. We gain an initial impression of a book once we know its genre, and its genre guides us in how we read it.

One evening I sat down with a book and was hooked by this opening sentence: "As Gregor Samsa awoke from an uneasy sleep, he found himself transformed into a gigantic insect." It was a striking sentence, but it didn't shake me. The book was *Metamorphosis*, by Franz Kafka, a story in which human beings can turn into bugs. I was able to suspend my disbelief because I knew I was immersing myself in fiction.

The Bible is a cornucopia of literary types. It reminds me of my mother's Thanksgiving dinner table. She used a special centerpiece on that special day when we'd celebrate God's material blessings. She would set a wicker horn—a cornucopia—in the center of the table and fill it with small pumpkins, gourds, and ornamental corn that overflowed onto the tablecloth. As we open the Bible's pages we encounter a spiritual cornucopia—a gift from God for our spiritual nourishment—in a diversity of writings that command our interest, stimulate our imaginations, and address every aspect of our lives.

As we read from Genesis to Revelation, we move through history, law, poetry, wisdom, prophecy, gospels, epistles, and apocalyptic literature. And when we know the type—the genre—of the literature we're reading, we can understand it better. We read history differently from how we read poetry. Different genres evoke different expectations and interpretive strategies.

Genre is such an important concept for proper reading of the Scriptures that we're going to devote the rest of this book to exploring the main types of biblical literature. In turn, we'll examine how history, law, wisdom and poetry, prophecy and apocalyptic, gospel and parable, and letters should be interpreted. Each leads us, in different ways, to an encounter with Jesus Christ.

Principle 4: Consider the historical and cultural background of the Bible. The Bible was written in a time and culture far different from ours. So, to discover the author's meaning, we must learn to read as if we were one of his contemporaries.

How do we do this? Most of us turn to commentaries and other helps. These books can provide insight into the cultural and historical backgrounds of the biblical writings. For example, the Bible often depicts the Lord as riding a cloud (see Psalm 18:7-15, 104:3, Nahum 1:3). A commentary would tell us that Israel's neighbors frequently pictured their god, Baal, riding a chariot into battle. As we place the biblical image in the light of the ancient Near East, we realize that God's cloud is a chariot He rides into war. When we turn to the New Testament and see that Jesus is also a cloud rider (Matthew 24:30, Revelation 1:7), we understand that this is not a fluffy white cloud but a storm cloud He rides into judgment. We now sense that the Old Testament imagery was calling Baal-worshiping Israelites to come back and worship the true cloud rider, Yahweh (God's proper name in the Old Testament, often translated LORD).

What about a passage like Psalm 23:1? Can't we understand the imagery of a shepherd without recourse to the ancient world? We know what a shepherd does; he protects, guides, and takes care of his sheep.

The answer is yes—and no. Shepherds in biblical times acted like shepherds in modern times in all these ways. But if we aren't aware of the use of the shepherd image in the ancient Near East, we will miss an important aspect of the psalm. The kings of the Near East often referred to themselves as the "shepherds" of their people. As we read Psalm 23 in the light of its ancient background, we recover an important teaching: The Lord is a *royal* shepherd.

Principle 5: Pay attention to the grammar and structure within a passage. We must read our passage closely, in all its grammatical detail. We need to see how the thought of the author progresses. We need to follow his argument, enter his story world, absorb his poetry. To do this, we look for things like connectors (such as *but* and *therefore*), verb tenses, and noun modifiers to help us uncover the logical connections between ideas.

Let's look at conjunctions, tenses, adjectives, and other indications of relationship in a few sentences of Psalm 131. Our example is from a poem that has a special kind of structural feature—parallelism—in which the clauses echo each other. The first clause makes a statement, which is then expanded in the following clauses. When you read any biblical poem, reflect on how the parallelism contributes to the meaning. Here, the parallel structure (both in the meaning of the words and the grammar) links the first three clauses of verse 1:

> My heart is not proud, O LORD,
>> my eyes are not haughty;
> I do not concern myself with great matters
>> or things too wonderful for me.

Careful attention to the structural relationship between the three clauses shows that David distances himself from pride in three distinct areas: his core personality (heart), his external demeanor (eyes), and his actions.

The *but*, which begins the next verse, draws a strong contrast between the pride described in the first verse and the attitude expressed in the second.

> But I have stilled and quieted my soul;
> like a weaned child with its mother
>> like a weaned child is my soul within me.

The English translation of the Hebrew verbs ("have stilled" and "have quieted") indicate that David's confidence was rooted in the past and continued in the present. He then illustrated his present disposition by using the word *like*. Note that David didn't use a generic term for "child"; rather, he used the word for "weaned child." When we reflect on the word choice, we realize that a weaned child doesn't need its mother's milk and is calm on its mother's lap. The child isn't grasping for the source of its sustenance but resting quietly in its mother's arms.

The final verse of the psalm uses imperatives to drive home the truths presented in the first two verses:

> O Israel, put your hope in the LORD
>> both now and forevermore.

Serious grammatical and syntactical (structural) study must be based on the original languages. Most Bible readers can't read the Hebrew text of the Old Testament or the Greek of the New Testament. For that reason, it's helpful to have a copy of a very literal translation, such as *The New American Standard Bible*, for serious study. Again, the best way to get a feel for the original text is to compare a number of translations. Also, a good commentary based on the Hebrew or Greek text is invaluable for insight into the grammatical and structural relationships.

Principle 6: Interpret experience in the light of Scripture, not vice versa. All too often, we distort the Bible's meaning by allowing our experiences to shape our understanding of a passage rather than the other way around. Many readers take a passage out of context to support their doctrinal theories, ignore the rest of the Bible's teaching, and argue that their "truth" is the same as biblical truth.

For instance, if sharing my faith makes me uncomfortable, I could build an excuse for not doing evangelism around the biblical passages that speak of God's love. I could quote 1 Corinthians 13 and a host of other passages to show that God and love are nearly synonymous. Then I might reason: "If God is love, how could He condemn anybody to an eternity in hell?" In this way, I would be "off the hook" for not telling people about Jesus, despite all the clear biblical teaching about sin, judgment, and hell.

Another way our experience can warp interpretation is when we unconsciously lay our Western values on biblical texts as we read. For instance, capitalism, as such, is nowhere taught in the Bible; neither is socialism. But American right-wing Christians and Latin American proponents of liberation theology might use the Bible to promote their political agendas. The antidote to such lopsided reading is to point to biblical passages that undermine both capitalism and socialism in the Bible. A white, middle-class experience of capitalism as good and socialism as bad should not lead to thinking the former is biblical and the latter unbiblical.

Perhaps one of the most hotly debated issues in evangelical circles today is whether certain gifts of the Spirit, such as prophecy and speaking in tongues, continue today. Arguments on both sides of this debate often appeal to experience over biblical teaching. If someone speaks in tongues, she will be predisposed to believe the Bible justifies the experience — "I can't deny what God has done in my life!" If someone else observes that in some settings these gifts bring chaos to worship, he might be more likely to find evidence to refute the practice — "How can God be the author of this confusion?"

It's difficult, but we must constantly strive to interpret our experience in the light of Scripture, rather than using our experience to make the Bible say only what we'd like it to say.

Principle 7: Always seek the full counsel of Scripture. We should never read Bible passages in isolation from the whole teaching of Scripture. Although many human authors contributed to the Bible, God is the ultimate Author of the whole. And while the Bible is an anthology of many books, it is also one book. The Bible has many stories to tell, but they all contribute to a single story. So we must read a passage, a chapter, or even a book of the Bible in context with the body of teaching and doctrine that flows from the complete history of God's progressive revelation in the Word.

This principle has many important implications. First, we won't base doctrine or moral teaching on an obscure passage. The most important ideas in the Bible are stated more than once. When a text appears to teach something obscure or questionable, and we can't find other passages to support it, we must not attach too much significance to it.

Second, if one passage *seems* to teach something, but another passage clearly teaches something else, we must seek to understand the difficult passage in light of the one that is easier to understand. That is, we can determine the meaning of the unclear verse by examining the clear teaching of Scripture.

Remember the radio Bible teacher I debated on the subject of Christ's return? The debate never would have happened if he and his supporters had simply applied the principle of seeking the full counsel of Scripture. You see, they produced all kinds of convoluted mathematical arguments, based on obscure portions of Scripture, which led them to believe Christ would return in 1994. The clear teaching of Scripture refutes the teacher's approach. Take a look at Mark 13:32: "No one knows about that day or hour." Just reading that verse should have stopped all the manipulating of passages to reach a faulty conclusion.

To grasp the full counsel of Scripture, we need to study the themes and analogies that stretch from Genesis to Revelation. Then, when we read any one passage, we will be able to understand its place in the unfolding history of salvation. This principle is particularly important as we read the Old Testament. Jesus said that the entire Old Testament, not just a handful of messianic prophecies, anticipated His coming (see Luke 24:25-27, 44).

In this regard, look at Matthew 4:1-11, which describes Jesus' temptation in the wilderness. If we keep the whole of Scripture in mind as we read, this reference may remind us of the Israelites' forty-year trek in the wilderness. But the comparison goes beyond the number forty. The Israelites also were tempted in the wilderness in the same three areas in which Jesus was tempted: hunger and thirst, testing God, and worshipping false gods. Jesus shows Himself to be the obedient Son of God where the Israelites were disobedient. Indeed, Jesus responded to the temptations by quoting Deuteronomy, the sermon Moses gave the Israelites at the end of their forty-year sojourn.

Reading Scripture in the light of the whole message, the whole counsel of God, not only prevents erroneous interpretations, it gives us deeper insight into the Word of God.

READY FOR THE CHALLENGE?

In light of all we have said about hermeneutical principles, I hope you are inspired to move into the Word with a new vigor, with a heart overflowing in new anticipation. Yet as we've seen, interpretation isn't necessarily an easy task. On one level we could call it quite challenging, for the same book that gently invites us to step into healing waters of spiritual life might cause us significant anxiety; we're tempted to remain on the shore in fear of certain swirling "interpretive rapids." Writer Fredrick Buechner eloquently summarizes this paradox, describing both the daunting challenge and the compelling attraction the Bible is for us:

> [We could say that] . . . it is a disorderly collection of sixty-odd books which are often tedious, barbaric, obscure, and teem with contradictions and inconsistencies. It is a swarming compost of a book, an Irish stew of poetry and propaganda, law and legalism, myth and murk, history and hysteria. Over the centuries it has become hopelessly associated with tub-thumping evangelism and dreary piety, with superannuated superstition and blue-nosed moralizing, with ecclesiastical authoritarianism and crippling literalism . . .
>
> And yet—
>
> And yet just because it is a book about both the sublime and the unspeakable, it is a book also about life the way it really is. It is a book about people who at one and the same time can be both believing and unbelieving, innocent and guilty, crusaders and crooks, full of hope and full of despair.
>
> In other words, it is a book about us.[1]

It's true. In spite of all its potentially confusing variety of styles and themes, the Bible presents one story and a simple message— a story all about us, all about God's love for us. He made us, but we sinned and broke fellowship with Him. He pursued us and provided our salvation by sending His Son to die on the cross in our place. And God raised Him from the dead that we might believe in Him and follow Him the rest of our lives.

We might think of the Word as a diamond—a single jewel with many facets. We can look through one of its facets and still see the same diamond but from a slightly different perspective. God tells us the one great story through different types of writings that reflect life's breadth and richness.

The most important thing to remember as you approach the Bible is to come to it with an openness to hear God speaking directly to your heart. He cares about you and your deepest concerns. Don't allow principles or guidelines to take away the power of your encounter with Him. But do use them as a guide for accurate interpretation.

In the following chapters we'll explore the different genres God has chosen for speaking to our hearts and minds. We'll describe each and point out where in the Bible we can discover them. We'll learn the proper way to read each genre to ensure that we're getting God's intended message. And we'll reflect on why God found these particular types of writings appropriate to communicate His message of salvation and spiritual transformation through Jesus Christ.

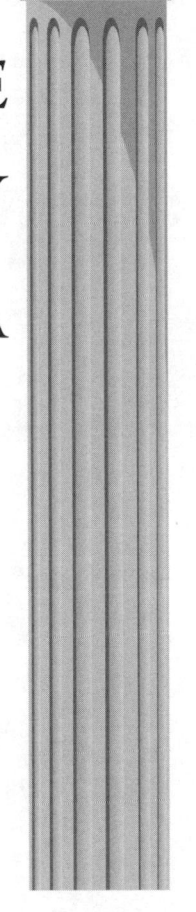

PART IV

THE
LITERARY
CORNUCOPIA

8
READING
IT AFRESH

"Who would ever know?" Michael muttered to himself, as he drove at a good clip down the interstate. The conference was miles from home, and he was the only representative attending from his company. This client not only could give him substantial business, she was very attractive, and she was obviously coming on to him. Her husband had dumped her, so no one would get hurt.

So why am I feeling so uneasy? He kept seeing the faces of his friends back in church, and it gave him a pang in the pit of his stomach. Of course, they were all married and presumably didn't have to deal with the kind of sexual tension he was facing.

And many of them had studied the life of Joseph with him in a home Bible class. *A woman threw herself at him too,* Michael recalled. But Joseph resisted. Something about offending God.

But look what his obedience got him—jail time! And that was ancient history. Back then it was a big deal to sleep around; now everybody does it. As he continued to drive, Michael reached for another antacid . . .

LIVING IN HISTORY

Struggling with conscience can give any of us a stomachache. And we know that the Bible, conveying principles of godly living, can build within us a moral hedge that's tough to hurdle (guilt free, at least).

What parts of the Bible help us live right? All the parts! At first blush, though, you might not pick the genre of biblical history as the most compelling portion when it comes to spiritual formation.

Actually, history is the most common type of literature found in the Bible. When we think of history in the Bible, our minds go first to books like Genesis, Exodus, Leviticus . . . all the way through Esther. Or we think of the Acts of the Apostles in the New Testament. Even the books of the Bible that aren't strictly history often have a solid connection with it. The prophets spoke from a specific historical moment and even the wisdom of Job has a historical setting. With this in mind, do you see how important it is to learn how to read history in the Bible?

We are the only creatures God has created with an awareness of the past. Our Christian faith grows out of confidence in past events, especially Jesus' death and resurrection. Their life-changing significance for our present gives us hope for the future.

The psalmist recognized the importance of the past in his relationship with God. Hear him in this poetic outpouring:

> O my people, hear my teaching;
>   listen to the words of my mouth.
> I will open my mouth in parables,
>   I will utter hidden things, things from of old—
> what we have heard and known,
>   what our fathers have told us.
> We will not hide them from their children;
>   we will tell the next generation
> the praiseworthy deeds of the LORD,
>   His power, and the wonders he has done.
> He has statutes for Jacob
>   and established the law in Israel,

which he commanded our forefathers
    to teach their children,
so the next generation would know them,
    even the children yet to be born,
    and they in turn would tell their children.
Then they would put their trust in God
    and would not forget his deeds
    but would keep His commands.
They would not be like their forefathers—
    a stubborn and rebellious generation,
whose hearts were not loyal to God,
    whose spirits were not faithful to him. (Psalm 78:1-8)

This psalm continues for another sixty-five verses, recounting the history of Israel during the wilderness wanderings, the first faltering steps of the monarchy under Saul, and concluding with David's rise to the kingship. We'll concentrate on this psalm's "prelude"—which is Psalm 77—because it gives wonderful insight into the practical importance of history in the Bible.

A BULWARK OF HOPE FOR TODAY

History is geared to the present and the future. The psalmist recounts the events of the past for his generation and for future ones represented by the community's children. If the children are faithfully to follow the God who has helped their elders in the past, they will have to learn the lessons of history.

These lessons will lead them to certain behaviors in the present. Most significantly, it will lead them to "put their trust in God." In other words, history builds faith. If God has saved us from suffering and trouble in the past, He can certainly do so in the present.

A good friend of mine, John, learned this lesson as he struggled with his eldest teenage daughter, Samantha. He loved her with all his heart and trusted her implicitly. But when she was fifteen, she was arrested for shoplifting. John couldn't understand it. Samantha was secure at home, well provided for, smart, athletic, had lots of friends. When she was arrested and given six months probation, John's world came tumbling down around him.

A few months later John received a call from school. Samantha had been caught drinking on campus, and she was suspended. John's initial reaction was to question God's love and concern for him and his daughter. Her rebellion was dragging the whole family down.

Then a friend of John's encouraged him to read Psalm 77. When he read these words of Scripture, he felt as though the psalmist had put a wiretap on his brain waves. The psalm expressed in detail his feelings of anxiety and depression and his sense that God had abandoned him in his present trouble (verses 3-9).

But the writer didn't end on a note of wrenching despair. In the middle of the psalm (verses 10-12), he remembered that God was in the business of helping people who felt as though they were on the brink of collapse. He remembered those many times in the past when God had rescued His people, just when they least expected it. The psalmist's faith and hope blossomed anew when he looked into the past and remembered, in particular, the Exodus (verses 16-20), the time when God rescued Israel from certain death at the hands of an angry pharaoh. By divine intervention the Red Sea had split wide open.

John's faith and hope grew as he, too, remembered times when God had reached out to him just when it seemed as though he had no strength to continue. For biblical history is, indeed, a bulwark of hope for God's people. God, in contrast to us and the animals, has no beginning and no end. But the first thing the Bible shows us is that God doesn't hover above us in some kind of transcendent, timeless sense; rather, He has chosen to enter our fallen world to speak with us. We see this most dramatically in the incarnation of Jesus Christ:

> Who, being in very nature God,
>> did not consider equality with God something to be
>> grasped,
> but made himself nothing,
>> taking the very nature of a servant,
>> being made in human likeness. (Philippians 2:6-7)

God has entered our finite space and time to interact with us. The history genre of God's Word narrates His involvement with us in our everyday world.

REAL SPACE AND TIME

Early Jewish tradition divided the Old Testament into three parts: the Law (the "instruction books," also called the Torah), the Prophets, and the Writings. Most of the books we call history are found in the first and second parts. The Prophets are also divided into two sections: the Former Prophets (Joshua, Judges, Samuel, Kings) and the Latter Prophets (Isaiah, Jeremiah, Ezekiel and the twelve Minor Prophets).

When we note the close connection between the "history" books and prophets like Isaiah, we get our first hint that these books are not textbook history but prophetic or theological history. Though grounded in real space and time, their purpose isn't simply to give a list of important events of the past. They bear witness to God's acts in the past. They tell us what He has done so we will draw closer to Him. They give us courage to face the difficulties of the present and hope to walk into an uncertain future.

Prophetic history doesn't mean "made-up" history, however. The events of the Bible are as real as what happened to you today. So the first important principle of reading the historical books, or any book of the Bible that intends to teach history, is to *learn how God treated His people in space and time in previous generations.*

When we read about the Exodus from Egypt, for example, we read about an occurrence that truly happened in the distant past. The author[1] wants to share something that took place during his lifetime in order to benefit others. Remember Michael at the beginning of this chapter? As Michael struggled with sexual desire and opportunity during a business trip, his mind (and stomach) were disturbed by recalling how Joseph rejected the sexual advances of Potiphar's wife (Genesis 39). This event actually took place. Joseph, a real person, was propositioned by a powerful woman who, when rejected, falsely accused him and landed him in jail. Michael's conscience was pricked by something that had happened thousands of years before.

Because the Bible's history books tell us what really happened in the past, we may find help in reading contemporary extrabiblical writings and archeology. For more than a century scholars have been engaged in the archaeological exploration of Israel and other lands of the Bible (primarily Jordan, Syria, Lebanon, Iraq, Iran, Turkey, Italy, and Egypt). They've discovered quite a bit in terms of ancient artifacts, architecture, and writings.

The writings, in particular, have proven helpful to our reading of the biblical text. Often these writings can fill out the historical record in ways that enrich our reading. For instance, the book of Nahum predicts the end of the great Assyrian city of Nineveh. We can get a sense of the power and greatness of that city by reading about the modern archaeological site now identified as ancient Nineveh.[2] From various chronicles of the Babylonians who defeated the city, we get a fuller picture of

Nahum's time period as well as the way in which God fulfilled the prophecy against Nineveh. Scholar D. J. Wiseman has published a number of Babylonian documents that include a mention of the taking of the city of Nineveh.[3] Most readers will find this kind of material conveniently presented in a good Bible commentary.[4]

On occasion, the archaeological and ancient Near Eastern literature will confirm the truth of the biblical text as well as fill in some missing information. For years the historical reliability of Daniel had been doubted on the grounds that it reports the last king of Babylon as Belshazzar. From other historical reports outside the Bible, the last king was a man named Nabonidus. Confirmation of the biblical text came when more ancient Near Eastern documents were discovered, revealing that Nabonidus placed his son Belshazzar on the throne while he moved for a long period of time to the southern part of his kingdom.[5]

Not only was the name Belshazzar explained in this way, but Daniel 5:16 became clear. In this verse, Belshazzar told Daniel that if he interpreted the writing on the wall, the king would make him third most powerful in the kingdom. Why third, rather than second? Because Nabonidus and his son Belshazzar were joint kings!

Why does the Bible give us so many extensive historical accounts? One big reason is that *God acted in history* to save us; therefore, our faith is grounded in space-and-time events. The gospel of Luke (a historical text) gives its purpose quite clearly in its first verses:

> Many have undertaken to draw up an account of the things that have been fulfilled among us, just as they were handed down to us by those who from the first were eyewitnesses and servants of the word. Therefore, since I myself have carefully investigated everything from the beginning, it seemed good also to me to write an orderly account for you, most excellent Theophilus, so that you may know the certainty of the things you have been taught. (Luke 1:1-4)

The purpose of the book of Luke is to present a reasoned and accurate account of what really happened during Jesus' life. Since Luke was probably originally linked with Acts, we can see that another purpose was to tell what happened during the first years after Jesus' death and resurrection.

But the history genre, like other genres, has a larger purpose: Its intent is to teach us about God and our relationship with Him.

HISTORY AS THEOLOGY

No one can write history from a purely objective point of view. After all, every person is a subject, not an object, and therefore everyone infuses subjectivity into his or her work. Any historian will write from a definite perspective with certain biases. Just compare a book on the American Revolution written in America with one written in England! On occasion a history account may be distorted to the point that it is false. Take, for instance, neo-Nazi efforts to convince the world that the Holocaust never happened.

So it's important to remember that all history reporting, ancient and modern, adopts a viewpoint through which the past is evaluated. And the person recounting the history can't tell us everything. He can only write about a small number of events from the vast and complex number that actually took place. Historians must make decisions about what's important and what's not, about what deserves to survive in our memory and what will be forgotten.

Furthermore, historians have to make decisions about causation. *Why* did something occur? Why did a king or political leader behave in the way he did? Writers of history not only choose to record certain events and not others, they also give those events a spin. That is, they interpret the events. Here's what the author of the gospel of John tells us about Jesus' life:

> This is the disciple who testifies to these things and who wrote them down. We know that his testimony is true. Jesus did many other things as well. If every one of them were written down, I suppose that even the whole world would not have room for the books that would be written. (John 21:24-25)

John, under the inspiration of the Spirit, had to pick and choose from among the many possible topics and events in Jesus' life. What would he include? As we will quickly see, one of the most productive approaches to the study of biblical history books is to ask what issues and concerns fuel and guide their authors' choices.

The historical writers of the Bible not only chose what to include, they also interpreted the events. The purpose of the Bible, after all, is to give glory to God. So it reports events showing how God is working in the world, that its readers might indeed bring honor to His name.

AN HISTORIC BREAKTHROUGH

Our faith is grounded in the veracity of the events recorded in God's Word. Nowhere is this more true than in the case of two critical reports: the crucifixion and resurrection of Christ. As Paul stated, "If Christ has not been raised, our preaching is useless and so is your faith" (1 Corinthians 15:14). Our faith has its roots planted in the bedrock of what really happened, not in the loose topsoil of myth, dream, or legend. And this body of "what really happened" has all been faithfully passed down to us through the generations because the birth, life, and ministry of Jesus was the most miraculous breakthrough in human history. No wonder His disciples passed it along—they had experienced it firsthand. And we are related to them by what we, too, have experienced of the same living Lord.

> [The disciples] found others who had already shared their experience. It is the glory of the Christian that he lives in a fellowship of people who have had the same experience as he has had.
>
> It has been said that true friendship begins only when people share a common memory and can say to each other, "Do you remember?" Each of us is one of a great fellowship of people who share a common experience and a common memory of their Lord.[6]

The history books reveal more to us than God's existence; they are a testimony to God's patient love for His people down through the ages. He shows us that He breaks through to our lives. He encounters us human beings in history in order to change us. And He brings us into fellowship with all who have experienced His gracious salvation. Our experience and memory of history, then, is our most foundational bond of unity.

Specifically, how do the history books contribute to our spiritual formation? As we turn to the next chapter we'll see that these books do not simply inform. They are sermons that illustrate principles of godly living and point us to Jesus Christ, the One who is at the center of all history.

9

LEARNING THE LESSONS OF THE PAST

How does biblical history affect our thinking and actions today? How is it a mirror that reflects our soul and a seed that transforms our lives? In the story that began our last chapter, Michael was tempted to engage in an affair. However, his recollection of Joseph and Potiphar's wife (Genesis 39) kept him from following through on his desire. This ancient example from the past sent up a spiritual flare in Michael's heart, just as if someone had encountered him in the midst of his struggle and preached a powerful sermon applying directly to his life. Ultimately, he resisted the temptation of an affair.

HISTORY PREACHES A SERMON

Yes, we might say that the biblical books of history are long sermons in story form, with the "preacher's text" being the actual events of history. The biblical authors recount the events to teach their contemporary generations and future ones about God and about life. Each author describes what has happened. In some cases we have to find the significance for our lives ourselves; in other cases, the biblical author reveals that significance to us.

Paul affirmed the value history has in the present in 1 Corinthians 10:1-3 as he remembered the Israelites' Red Sea crossing and wandering in the wilderness. He went on to say, "Now these things occurred as examples to keep us from setting our hearts on evil things as they did" (verse 6). Thus Paul instructs us to read the history of the Bible for theology and ethics as well, and to glean lessons of godly behavior. For example, we can look at the life of Abraham in the book of Genesis as a lesson in the ups and downs of faith.

God tells Abraham to leave his homeland and God would bless him with children—"I will make you into a great nation"—and give him a land of his own (Genesis 12:1-3). Abraham obeys and leaves comfortable Ur for unknown Canaan. When he arrives, the land—the Promised Land—is experiencing a famine. So Abraham must go to Egypt. Does he trust God to protect him, guide him, and provide for him? No, he fears for his life and tells his wife Sarah to lie about her relationship with him for fear that Pharaoh will kill him (12:10-20). Not a pretty picture of faith in God's promises!

In the next episode (13:1-18), we see that Abraham does trust God. Indeed, he has so much confidence in God's ability to give him the land that he doesn't fight with Lot or manipulate him; he allows Lot to choose which part of the land he will use.

God tells us Abraham's story to keep a record of the past and to encourage us in our own faith journeys. In this way, we can understand what is going on in our own souls and be stimulated to pursue God more passionately. Recalling this Old Testament story, why not take a moment right now to read Hebrews 11:8-12,17-19? Think about how it all applies to your own life. In other words, if someone were to ask you how the story of Abraham affects you today, what would you say? Do you see anything of Abraham's fear in your own soul? Have you sometimes acted just as courageously as he did on God's behalf? What insight about your relationship with God springs from your thinking? What kinds of prayer?

Note that God also records examples of ungodly behavior in biblical history. The story of Ahab in 1 Kings 21 is a good example. King Ahab wants a nice little plot of ground near the palace for a royal vegetable garden. But the land belongs to Naboth, who doesn't want to give it up. Kings were powerful, but God had given every Israelite a bit of the Promised Land, and not even the king was allowed to take it.

King Ahab was married to Jezebel, a foreign princess, and she encouraged Ahab to defraud Naboth out of his God-given land. They were successful in their plot. But soon God's prophet appeared and condemned their actions, illustrating how bad it is to use personal and political power to cheat someone out of what is rightfully his.

These are clear examples of ways we can apply biblical history to our lives for spiritual growth. But at this point, you may be wondering, "Can I apply everything I read in the history books?"

Clearly, we do need to exercise some caution as we think about contemporary applications of Old Testament stories. We can't assume that everything recorded is an example given to us for our spiritual growth. We must take into account that *what happened in the past might have occurred under special circumstances* and no longer applies to us.

For instance, we may marvel at the story of Joshua fighting the Canaanites and then make the mistake of identifying our nation's armed forces with the Israelite army, concluding that whenever we go to war we're fighting a holy cause with God on our side. The "holy war" was a phenomenon of the Old Covenant when the people of God were one nation. Today the people of God are scattered throughout many nations and our holy war is now a spiritual conflict, not a physical one (see Ephesians 6:10-20).

The best safeguard against misapplying historical material is to find support from a passage that teaches the principle in a straightforward way. Genesis 39, the story of Joseph resisting the seduction of Potiphar's wife, is a clear example of godly morality because of the consistent teaching throughout Scripture that adultery is wrong. In addition to this safeguard, we must not lose sight of the loftier purpose of the biblical histories. They are more than a mirror and seed. Through them God tells us the story of salvation—His unfolding plan to bring people into relationship with Himself. That history climaxes in Christ Jesus.

HISTORY POINTS TO JESUS

We've already seen that Jesus' own statements affirmed the witness of the Old Testament to His coming in such passages as Luke 24:25-27, 44-49. But where do we find these foreshadowings of Him?

God has worked out our salvation in history, and He has told us what He has done through the Bible. God is not only the ultimate author of the Bible; He is also the ultimate author of history. We shouldn't be too surprised, then, to discover that the historical events of the Old Testament reverberate throughout history and find their most dramatic expression in the life of Christ. To see this more clearly, let's take a look at the Exodus from Egypt.

The Exodus, the actions of God rescuing His people from harsh slavery, is the most important salvation event of the Old Testament. After His people crossed the Red Sea, God continued to watch over the Israelites for forty years as they wandered in the wilderness. During this time, He made them a nation and gave them the Ten Commandments and the rest of the Law. At the end of the forty years He fought on their behalf, displacing the Canaanites from Palestine and giving the Israelites their own homeland.

These events happened in time and space, and the books of Exodus through Joshua recount them to warn and encourage later generations of God's people. Early on we get hints that God has presented a pattern of salvation that will be repeated — as an ever-resounding echo — finally culminating in Jesus Christ. The earliest hint of this echoing comes in Joshua 3 and 4.

Echoes of the Exodus throughout the Old Testament. With the exception of Joshua and Caleb, the entire first generation that witnessed the miraculous crossing of the Red Sea had died. The new generation, standing at the Jordan River, was about to learn that God was still with them and still powerful. As they took their first step into the Promised Land, the waters of the Jordan stopped flowing. In a reprise of the Red Sea crossing, the entire nation marched into the Promised Land over a dry river bed.

Yet, from the viewpoint of spiritual growth, we can't celebrate Israel's occupation of the land with unqualified enthusiasm. They messed things up quite often! They repeatedly betrayed the Lord. By the eighth century B.C., many centuries after the historical Exodus, prophets like Isaiah and Hosea began to predict that God's punishment would fall on the people once again. God's chosen people would be removed from the land, said the prophets. Many would be killed, but others would spend their lives in a foreign country. In effect, the Israelites would experience a second slavery, this time in Babylon.

But God also gave the prophets a vision that extended beyond the punishment. They spoke of a remnant who would return to the land and restore it in the future. The language they used to describe this return echoed the earlier Exodus and wilderness wanderings:

"Therefore I am now going to allure her;
    I will lead her into the desert
    and speak tenderly to her.
There I will give her back her vineyards,
    and will make the Valley of Achor[1] a door of hope.
There she will sing as in the days of her youth,
    as in the day she came up out of Egypt." (Hosea 2:14-15)

Comfort, comfort my people,
    says your God.
Speak tenderly to Jerusalem,
    and proclaim to her
that her hard service has been completed,
    that her sin has been paid for,
that she has received from the LORD's hand
    double for all her sins.
A voice of one calling:
"In the desert prepare
    the way for the LORD;
make straight in the wilderness
    a highway for our God.
Every valley shall be raised up,
    every mountain and hill made low;
the rough ground shall become level,
    the rugged places a plain.
And the glory of the LORD will be revealed,
    and all mankind together will see it.
For the mouth of the LORD has spoken. (Isaiah 40:1-5)

These passages and others like them found their fulfillment in what we now call the second exodus—Israel's return to Palestine from Babylonian Exile, a process that began in 539 B.C.

Echoes of the Exodus in the life of Jesus. The echo extends beyond 539, as experienced Bible readers have already recognized. The gospel of Mark (1:2-3) begins with a quotation from the Isaiah passage. In effect, the opening of the gospel announces that some connection exists between the historical exodus and Jesus' ministry.

A brief survey of this rich comparison begins with the baptism of Jesus, which is His "Red Sea crossing." Paul called the Red Sea crossing the baptism of the Israelites (1 Corinthians 10:1-5). It was the beginning of their redemption, just as Jesus' baptism initiates His ministry.

After the crossing of the Red Sea, the Israelites wandered in the wilderness for forty years. Jesus, remarkably, goes into the wilderness for forty days and forty nights, where He is tempted by Satan (Matthew 4:1-11). More than a superficial numerical similarity is at work here. Jesus' temptations are the same as those the Israelites experienced in their wanderings. Jesus is tempted in regard to food; the Israelites complained heartily about their lack and quality of food. Jesus resists the temptation to test God; the Israelites were constantly testing God. Jesus rejects Satan's invitation to worship a false god; the Israelites caved in easily with the worship of a golden calf.

Jesus responds to Satan's temptations by quoting the book of Deuteronomy three times, using the speech Moses gave the Israelites just before his death and their entry into the Promised Land. Moses warned the people not to succumb to temptation as they had in the wilderness. Jesus, by resisting the temptations, shows that He is the obedient Son of God in precisely those areas where the Israelites had failed their heavenly Father.

This is just the beginning of the Exodus-echoes we find in Jesus. During the wilderness wanderings Moses went up on Mount Sinai and received the Law of God. It is more than a coincidence that in the gospel of Matthew (chapters 5-7) Jesus also went up a mountain, where He delivered a sermon on the law. Jesus was showing Himself to be the divine Lawgiver.

There are many more connections, but let's conclude by considering the end of Jesus' life. Jesus was crucified during the Passover (John 19:17-37); He became our Passover Lamb. What is the Passover but the Jewish festival that celebrates the Exodus (see Exodus 12)? The relationship is undeniable. The Gospels insist that we understand Jesus as the fulfillment of the Exodus.

Echoes of the Exodus in our lives today. As we continue to explore the books of biblical history, we'll see how our lives relate to the Exodus of old. The book of Hebrews informs us Christians that we are wandering in the wilderness, waiting to enter the Promised Land (Hebrews 3:7–4:13). We are pilgrims on earth who anticipate rest in the land, a clear allusion to heaven.

And who of us, in struggling with our sins and addictions, has not experienced the kind of cyclical journey that characterized the children of Israel in the Old Testament—a pattern of sin, repentance, redemption and falling into sin once again? Yet we can confidently hope that, as the cycle continues, it is gradually moving us in an upward spiral of spiritual growth. No doubt we are learning and

maturing and, little by little, divesting ourselves of the sin that "so easily entangles" us (see Hebrews 12:1-6). We have one more Jordan to
cross: the path from this life to the next. The history books, then, give
us a way to look at Jesus—the fulfillment of the Exodus—and also
a way to view our own lives as temporary pilgrimages. In our travels
through this life, we are to persevere on our way to something permanent and much more wonderful.

HISTORY TRANSFORMS OUR HISTORY

In a recent insightful article, Bible scholar Don Hudson encourages
us to "bring our story" to the Bible.[2] All of us have a story to tell. Even
if we don't keep a written record of our lives in the form of a journal
or diary, we keep a mental record that reads like a novel.

As you look to your past, what variety of characters dot your
mental landscape? Parents, children, spouse, play major roles; certain friends and acquaintances have walk-on parts. Some helped
you along the path of life; others threatened to undo you. You can
remember crucial events when your life took a turn for the better
or worse, as well as long expanses of uninterrupted routine. Such
details of our story all have to do with God's story. Though we may
often read the Bible only as interesting ancient tales of the past,
Hudson rightly reminds us that the biblical stories help us understand our own lives.

King David slept with Bathsheba and then covered up his sin by
having her husband, Uriah, killed. His actions don't seem to bother
him until he's confronted by the prophet Nathan (2 Samuel 11-12).
Perhaps we haven't sinned so boldly, but we read David's story and
recognize the deceit of our own hearts. We're then prodded by God
to turn to Him for forgiveness and transformation.

So we see that God informs us about the past for a present purpose. He wants us to know how He saved His people in the past so
that we, in the present, might put our confidence in Him. God knows
that the present often looks quite bleak. We look around and see
trouble brewing on all sides. We don't know how to get out of the
mess. But then we look back and see that God, time and time again,
saves His people from seemingly insurmountable odds. There is no
obstacle too great for our God!

What trouble is brewing in your life right now? Take some time
to read of God's deliverance in one or more of these historical
passages:

- Hagar's Fear (Genesis 21:8-20)
- Jacob's Struggle (Genesis 32:24-30)
- Joseph's Family Strife (Genesis 45–50:1)
- Manoah's Desire for a Son (Judges 13:1-7)
- David's Deliverance (2 Samuel 22:1,29-36)
- Daniel's Danger (Daniel 6)
- Mercy for Elizabeth (Luke 1:57-68,80)
- Some of your own favorites: _____

Ask yourself: *How do I relate to these people? In what ways do I experience the same hopes and fears, similar desires and motivations? What could God be telling me through their stories? What change in attitude or action will I attempt as a result?*

As you seek to apply the Bible directly to your own life, remember that history is the most pervasive of all the genres of the Bible. As you read it, keep these four principles in mind:

- History intends to inform us reliably about past events. Read them as a witness to how God has worked in time and space.
- History writers shape their presentation of the facts to make a point. The biblical history writers do so as well, inspired by God: they present the facts of history to glorify God in some special way. Look for the motivating questions and issues that drove the human authors of the book you are studying.
- Look for the *example* (1 Corinthians 10:6) the historical account provides. Are there things you can imitate in your own behavior? What things are you warned to avoid? Be sure to acknowledge the discontinuity between the Old and New Testaments while considering these questions.
- Always look for the connection to Christ. He is the center of history according to the Bible. All the events of the Old Testament anticipate the great act of redemption Jesus performed on the cross. The Bible is more than just a collection of isolated stories with important moral lessons. It tells one story. All the different stories — those of Abraham, Moses, David, Nehemiah, Daniel, the early church — contribute to the single story of God's salvation, and that story climaxes with Jesus Christ.

10

OBEYING THE GOD WHO SAVED US

At the end of my first year of college, two of my closest friends and I decided to room together. Dave and I had been Christians for about a year, and we were among the "mature" believers on campus. My closest friend from high school, Dan, now with me in college, had just become a Christian. We thought it would be exciting for the three of us to room together and have a Christian witness in our dorm.

There was only one problem. We needed a fourth roommate. Another close friend in the Christian fellowship came to us with the good news that her friend, Rodney, was transferring to our college. He was a Christian and the apparent answer to our prayers.

But not long after the semester began we started to wonder whether Rodney was the answer to our prayers—or a nightmare. Rodney would often come back to the room drunk or stoned. We heard reports of his sexual exploits on campus. At the same time, Rodney was amazing us all with his incredible knowledge of Scripture. None of us was even close to knowing the Bible like Rodney.

However, one evening Dan, Dave, and I returned from the library to discover Rodney in bed with a girl. We confronted him. "How can you consider yourself a Christian when you act worse than most of our nonChristian friends?"

His answer was illuminating as well as shocking, "The Bible says I'm saved by grace, not by works. How can you question my Christianity? It has absolutely nothing to do with how I behave, and God will forgive me anyway."

WHAT ABOUT THE LAW?

Rodney's view on law and grace is not as extreme a position as you might think. Many Christians wonder about what is right and what is wrong. They push the envelope with their lifestyles, and many more justify sinful behavior that is much less obvious. And while many Christians agree that the Ten Commandments still apply to their lives, they consign the rest of the Law's relevance to Old Testament times. After all, just as Rodney said: we're saved by faith and not by works.

But does the Law have anything to say to us today? Here's what Jesus said about it:

> "Do not think that I have come to abolish the Law or the Prophets; I have not come to abolish them but to fulfill them. I tell you the truth, until heaven and earth disappear, not the smallest letter, not the least stroke of a pen, will by any means disappear from the Law until everything is accomplished. Anyone who breaks one of the least of these commandments and teaches others to do the same will be called least in the kingdom of heaven, but whoever practices and teaches these commands will be called great in the kingdom of heaven. For I tell you that unless your righteousness surpasses that of the Pharisees and the teachers of the law, you will certainly not enter the kingdom of heaven." (Matthew 5:17-20)

These words clearly indicate the Law's continuing role for Christians. Within the context of salvation by faith, Paul affirmed,

"Do we, then, nullify the law by this faith? Not at all! Rather, we uphold the law" (Romans 3:31).

If the Law is applicable to our lives, do we have to eat only kosher food or dress in a certain way? Certainly we don't have to offer the sacrifices legislated by the book of Leviticus, do we? Before answering these questions, let's find out what, exactly, biblical law is and where it is found.

DETERMINING THE SCOPE OF THE LAW

The Bible contains many commands and imperatives, but not all of it is Law. By Law we refer specifically to the collection of requirements God imposed on Israel during the time of Moses. More than six hundred such laws, found in the Pentateuch (the first five books of the Old Testament), guided Israel's obedience to God.

We can't look at all the individual laws, so we'll describe Law under three headings. First, we'll look at the Ten Commandments and the so-called Book of the Covenant (Exodus 20:1–23:33, named in 24:7). Then we'll examine the laws of Leviticus and Numbers. In the next chapter we'll continue by exploring the laws of Deuteronomy, putting them in the context of ethical living today.

The Ten Commandments. This list of ethical prescriptions has first place in the Book of the Covenant and is likely the earliest collection of laws given to Israel. Moses ascended Mount Sinai to receive them etched in stone. All the other laws of the Book of the Covenant flow from the Ten Commandments.

Before giving the first commandment, God prefaces the law with this introduction: "I am the LORD your God, who brought you out of Egypt, out of the land of slavery" (Exodus 20:2). Note how this historical introduction links the Law to the history we discussed in the last chapter. God is the One who made Israel a people; He is the One who created their story and had a plan for them. Now He called on Israel to listen to Him for instructions about the way they should behave.

God's historical comment reminds the Israelites, and us, that His Law was not given so that they, or we, could be saved. God already did that! The laws that followed were the requirements for a people who wanted to live in a way that pleases their Savior. When we comment on the blessings and curses of the Law, we'll see that God's continued provision for Israel depended in large measure on Israel's obedience. But God's salvation was never dependent on His people's ability to keep the Law.

The Ten Commandments have an unusual form when compared with most other biblical laws (and almost all other ancient Near Eastern law). Most law takes the form "If then." It is case law. If one does a certain act or behaves in a certain way, then the specified consequences occur. In contrast, the Ten Commandments stand as absolute principles: "Honor your father and your mother" (20:12), "You shall not murder" (20:13), and the rest. All of them are the most basic requirements for God's people, that they might live in right relationship with Him and with each other. Traditionally, the Commandments have been divided into two parts: those that regulate our relationship with God (verses 3-11) and those that cover our relationship with others (verses 12-17).

The Ten Commandments are neither exhaustive in scope nor crystal-clear in application. For example, how would the sixth commandment—"Thou shalt not kill" (KJV)—apply in concrete situations? Did it mean the Israelites should not participate in war? What if a man's animal accidentally killed someone on his property? Would he be liable for murder?

The case law that flowed from the Ten Commandments applied the Commandments to particular situations in the community. Notice, for instance, the case law found in Exodus 21:28-29:

> If a bull gores a man or a woman to death, the bull must be stoned to death, and its meat must not be eaten. But the owner of the bull will not be held responsible. If, however, the bull has had the habit of goring and the owner has been warned but has not kept it penned up and it kills a man or woman, the bull must be stoned and the owner also must be put to death.

Here we can see how to apply the general principle concerning murder to a specific instance. Obviously, not all killing was considered murder, as shown by Exodus 22:2, a law that applied the eighth commandment—"Thou shalt not steal" (KJV). It says, "If a thief is caught breaking in and is struck so that he dies, the defender is not guilty of bloodshed."

The case law helps us apply the general laws of the Ten Commandments. But even the case law doesn't answer every specific question that might have come up in an ancient Israelite trial. What if the person killed by the ox had taunted it beforehand? What if it wasn't an ox that killed, but a ram? The application of the Law would have taken some thought during the Old Testament time period, not to speak of applying the Law today.

Notice that case law includes penalties. As we survey the various laws in the Book of the Covenant, we see that murdering (21:14), attacking one's father and mother (21:15), kidnapping (21:16), cursing one's parents (21:17), engaging in sorcery (22:18), practicing bestiality (22:19), worshiping false gods (22:20), and many other crimes demanded the death penalty. Conviction of theft must result in restitution (22:7-9).

Do such laws apply today? Do the penalties assigned to them apply today? We'll address these questions after a brief survey of the other collections of Law.

The Laws of Leviticus and Numbers. Leviticus and Numbers present a series of laws that supplement those found in the book of Exodus. These laws address specific topics when compared to the Book of the Covenant. The laws of Leviticus deal with sacrifices, cultic cleanliness, food, and the priesthood.

Most of the laws in these two books are the types of regulations that would especially apply to Old Testament priests. This is the case with the laws concerning sacrifice in Leviticus 1-7. They are probably directed to the priests, and their original purpose may well have been to inform priests, or to remind them, about how to perform certain sacrificial ceremonies (since there isn't much explanation about what the sacrifices meant). The priests knew what the sacrifices meant, and we can infer the theological significance of the various sacrifices from indirect comments.

Some of the laws in Leviticus that determined when a person was clean or unclean are hard for us to relate to today. For us, cleanness and uncleanness have to do with physical hygiene. For the ancient priests, it had to do with religious purity. To be clean meant to be in the right state to approach a powerful and holy God. To approach God in a state of uncleanness would mean certain doom.

Uncleanness was contagious in the sense that coming into contact with certain objects or people meant catching their uncleanness. Such objects and things were not necessarily sinful. They may have been excessively holy and protected by taboos. Blood and semen, two fluids that are crucial to sacrifice and to the fulfillment of the promise of descendants, were treated with special respect (Leviticus 15;17:10-12). Coming into contact with them rendered a person unclean because those substances were so important, not because they were dirty or sinful.

The laws detailing which foods were kosher (that is, clean) are a case in point (see Leviticus 11). Certain foods were prohibited, but not because they were considered unhealthy. It's more likely that the animals involved were viewed as not representing the pure species of creation. The clean animals had certain characteristics that the unclean animals lacked. For instance, land animals that could be eaten had to chew cud and have a split hoof (Leviticus 11:1-8). Camels, rabbits, and pigs didn't fit the bill.

The division of clean and unclean animals represented humanity, which was also divided into clean (Israelite) and unclean (Gentile). When the latter distinction was abolished because of the work of Christ, so was the former distinction.

READING THE LAW TODAY

The laws of Leviticus and Numbers raise special questions for Christian readers. How do they function as a seed that transforms us or a mirror that reflects our soul? After all, we no longer perform sacrifices, and the book of Hebrews informs us that Christ has offered Himself as the once-for-all sacrifice for our sins (Hebrews 10:1-18). As for the food laws, the New Testament explicitly states that all foods are clean. No longer are Jews and Gentiles distinct, so no longer are there laws separating clean and unclean foods (Acts 10:9-23,15). We know these laws had significance in the past, but what possible use do they have for the Christian today?

Certainly we can conclude that these laws no longer *directly* apply to us because of our place in the history of God's plan of salvation. Quite simply, we live in the period after Christ has come, while the Israelites of the Old Testament period anticipated that great event. As a result, many of the laws in the Old Testament are like these examples from Leviticus — they concern religious ceremonies that are fulfilled by Jesus Christ. Since Jesus has removed the wall that divides Jewish people and Gentiles (Ephesians 2:11-22), we no longer observe the food laws supporting that division. Since Jesus offered the sacrifice that was merely foreshadowed by animal sacrifices, we no longer perform such bloody rituals. (In the next chapter, however, we will see how they point us to Christ.)

Many of the laws of Leviticus and Numbers concern outward behavior — restricting what the people of God could eat, what they could wear, and so forth. The prophet Jeremiah told us that God was bringing a day when He would put His law "in their minds and write it on their hearts" (Jeremiah 31:33). Jesus told His disciples that He was not concerned with what goes into a person, but with what comes out (Mark 7:20). In other words, Jesus showed us what God really wants to cleanse and purify—our hearts. Christ's transforming work on the cross helps us to break free of desires that hold us in bondage. As we submit to God, we become like Christ, no longer wanting to offend God. Out of gratitude we obey Him from the inside out.

I once read of a situation among certain workers at a large motel on the Gulf Coast of Florida. It seems the management had made a rule that all employees must wear shoes during working hours, even if no one would see them as they cleaned the rooms and ran errands.

Some of the staff members who had not been around for very long complained bitterly about this. After all, during their break times they wanted to run out onto the beach, play in the sand, and wade in the surf. And they thought the soft, shag carpeting in the rooms would be easy on their feet, too. Everything would be so much more pleasant without "the crazy shoe rule."

A few of the other employees, those who had been around longer, viewed the rule in a different light. They knew that sometimes the late-night party crowd on the beach left broken bottles and other sharp objects hidden under a thin layer of sand. And some of these employees had run into stick pins in the carpeting or had skinned their toes on the sharp edges of bed frames. For them, the rule about shoes was much less a form of managerial harassment than a means of protection.

Whenever we confront a biblical "Don't," perhaps we should ask ourselves, "Are God's laws given just to spoil our fun? Or might they be one more sign that we have a loving heavenly Father who cares about us enough to guide us along the safest pathways in life?"

We might say that God's laws guard our lives. The Law continues to school us in what is right because our rebellious hearts would lead us into what would harm us and hurt others. And God cleanses our hearts of old desires by giving us the inner strength to obey. In Romans 7:21-25, Paul says that the struggle to obey never ends, but it does change as we grow in Christ. Our old nature transforms into our new nature (See 2 Corinthians 4:16).

There's more. While the Law no longer dictates our behavior, it serves as a reminder of our privileged status: we get to live during a time that was eagerly desired by the Old Testament faithful. We look back to the fulfillment of the Law in Jesus' crucifixion and resurrection, and the Law informs us of how great was His sacrifice for us. Now we can joyously offer our own "sacrifice of praise" to the Lord (Hebrews 13:15).

11

BEING FAITHFUL TO OUR DIVINE KING

As we've seen, Exodus, Leviticus, and Numbers raise a number of issues concerning God's Law and the modern Christian. Can we now totally ignore the Law? If not, what does our obedience to the Law look like today? We can't fully answer those questions before we look at the other major source of biblical law, the book of Deuteronomy.

BEING IN TREATY WITH GOD

Deuteronomy is Moses' final sermon before the Israelites take up residence in the Promised Land. Moses, because of an earlier sin, wasn't permitted to enter the land, so the thrust of his sermon was to encourage the people and warn them not to sin as they've been doing in the wilderness. But the laws (found mostly between chapters

5 and 26) come in the context of grace.

We can say this because, as we study the genre of the book, we see that it resembles an ancient Near Eastern treaty. Such treaties were formed when two countries wanted to enter into a relationship with one another. God, by using this form to speak to His people, steps into history to reveal Himself as Israel's king, showing the people how to relate to Him in a way that respects His glory and majesty. Specifically, the book of Deuteronomy follows the typical pattern of a treaty between a king who represents a powerful nation and the king of a relatively modest nation.[1] This type of relationship is called a vassal treaty (as opposed to a treaty of equals, called a parity treaty) and has at least six standard elements:

Introduction. A vassal treaty begins with the introduction of the two parties involved. In Deuteronomy 1 we do not have the actual treaty document, but we have an account of the ritual that affirms it. It's quite clear who the two parties are: God, who is the Great King, and the people of Israel, who are His servant people (1:1-5).

Historical review. An ancient treaty would often begin with a review of the history of the relationship between the two parties. In secular treaties, the great king would lay it on thick by telling the vassal king how wonderful he had been to the weaker nation and how ungrateful the other king had been to him. In Deuteronomy, of course, the historical remembrance is more than manipulative political ideology. It is the truth. God had been overwhelmingly gracious to Israel. From the Red Sea crossing to the moment forty years later when they stood poised to enter the Promised Land, God had taken care of His people (1:9–3:27).

Law-giving. After the gracious relationship between God and Israel has been firmly established, God gives them the Law. This, too, follows the pattern of the ancient Near Eastern treaties, in which the present obligations of the law spring from the relationship of the past. In Deuteronomy, though not in all biblical covenants, the Law takes up the lion's share of the content (4:1–26:19). Perhaps the reason for this is Moses' concern that Israel has been so disobedient in the wilderness.

The important theological point is that *God delivers the Law only after He has established His relationship with Israel.* The Law is not the cause of the relationship but the way in which the relationship will be continued and enriched. This is what we mean by saying the laws come in the context of grace. To make sure that Israel got its priorities straight, the Ten Commandments begin with this reminder, "I am the LORD your God, who brought you out of Egypt, out of the land of slavery" (Deuteronomy 5:6, Exodus 20:2). God had graciously acted on their behalf, prior to anything they could do to earn His benevolence.

Rewards and consequences. Next, the Law stipulates consequences for disobedience. In ancient Near Eastern treaties, the great king would inform the vassal that wonderful rewards would follow obedience to his laws, while punishment would surely reach the one who disobeyed. In a similar manner, conditions attach to Israel's response—either blessings or curses (27:1–28:68).

The blessings and curses of Deuteronomy make their presence felt throughout the canon of the Old Testament. Samuel and Kings, in particular, view the Exile as a result of breaking the Deuteronomic law, which brought on the dreaded curses. Deuteronomy 28:64 is an ominous anticipation of that horrible period of Israel's history when God promised disobedient Israel that He would "scatter [them] among all nations."

Witnesses. A treaty, being at heart a legal document, needs witnesses. In the ancient Near Eastern treaties, the gods and goddesses of the respective nations often served in this capacity. For Israel, the witness would be God's creation, heaven and earth itself (30:19-20).

Review and succession. To complete the picture of the treaty or covenant in Old Testament times, we must mention the concern for the treaty text itself (for example, where it should be placed) and regular reading of the document, as well as the provision for the succession of kings, especially in the vassal country. Treaties looked beyond the present to the future. Scribes made two copies of the treaty and usually placed them in the most important temples of the two nations entering the relationship.

This procedure wasn't necessary in the divine-human covenant, though it has been suggested that the two tablets of the Law are actually two copies. In either case, the Law was written and placed in the most sacred spot possible—the ark of the covenant. Every seven years, during the Feast of Tabernacles of the Jubilee Year, the priests would read the Law so the people could reaffirm their allegiance to it (31:9-13).

The laws of Deuteronomy illustrate what is true for law throughout the entire Bible—law comes *after* God's grace. God's people do not earn His love by obeying Him; they obey Him because they love Him. Thus Moses' final speech is actually the leading of his congregation, the Israelites, to reaffirm their relationship with the Lord. That relationship was sealed by covenant at Mount Sinai, and in Leviticus and Numbers they are reviewing it and saying, "Yes, we will continue to follow the Lord, even though we are entering a new and dangerous period of our national life."

What does it mean for us, today, that God's law comes in the form of a treaty? We must remember that we, too, live in covenant-treaty with God through Jesus Christ. Jesus established a new covenant with us based on His death and resurrection (Matthew 26:28, Mark 14:24, Luke 22:20). Jesus' heart was at rest in God, and ours can be too, because God has come to make a treaty with us.

Perhaps you don't realize this, at least on an experiential level. Perhaps you feel more as though you're at war with God. Just last night I heard the story of one of my students who grew up as a gang member in the inner-city of Philadelphia. He was confessing his feelings toward someone who had done some damage to his property. His first impulse was to get angry with God and revert to gang tactics. He felt at war with God and others.

Many people live as if they're not in a treaty relationship with God. Perhaps it's because the promise of peace, based on God's grace, also brings responsibility. How do we respond to this responsibility? Do we show our gratitude by keeping the Law given to Moses? To answer these questions, we need to first recognize the divisions of the laws of the Old Testament. They come to us in three different forms.

KNOWING THE DIFFERENCE

We can distinguish between three types of laws throughout the history of interpreting the Law. First, *ceremonial law* defines how Israel was to worship God. An example would be the laws commanding and describing the ritual for the sacrifice of a whole burnt offering (Leviticus 1). Other ceremonial laws included the laws regulating the priesthood and the place of worship, as well as the festivals that celebrated Yahweh's great acts in history.

Second are the *civil laws*. These laws regulated Israel as a nation chosen by God to be His special people. For instance, Deuteronomy 17:14-20 tells the people how they should choose a king. The office of king isn't defined because it's assumed the king will have the same powers and authorities as the "nations around" Israel. However, this power is limited, since the king is to be a reflection of a far greater King—God. Kings, therefore, were not to abuse their powers by taking many wives or amassing personal wealth. On the positive side, a king was to be an avid student of God's Word as a leader of the people. Such laws were crucial for Israel. As a nation, they were to reflect God's power and love to all the nations.

Today there are no chosen nations in the sense that Israel was then the chosen nation of God, and therefore the Old Testament's civil laws do not directly apply to the present. While certain principles may be applied to the present (for instance, a desire for strong moral character in our political leaders), certainly the Law as a whole does not apply in detail to us. For example, even though God's people had a king over them, that doesn't mean Christians today should lobby for a king instead of a president. Neither must we refrain from voting if no Christian candidate is in the running.

The third division, *moral law,* states God's principles of a right relationship with Him and with others. The Ten Commandments are the most visible and powerful expression of God's will to His people, and as we read the New Testament and reflect on the Bible as a whole, we see that these commands are still operative. Jesus approved of the following summary of the Ten Commandments: "'Love the Lord your God with all your heart and with all your soul and with all your strength and with all your mind'; and 'Love your neighbor as yourself'" (Luke 10:27).

Much of the civil law that flows from the Ten Commandments gives specific applications to the people of God centuries ago, in their sociological setting. The law of the goring ox, which we cited above, applies the principle "Do not murder" to a specific culture. The law to build a fence around a roof is a practical application of the same commandment (Deuteronomy 22:8). The roof was a living area in ancient Israel. Neglecting to build a fence on the roof might cause injury or death for careless family members or friends.

This raises an interesting question concerning moral law that is made specific in case law. The moral law is still relevant but must be applied to our own time and culture. While it would seem ridiculous to build a fence around every roof since we do not use our roofs as ancient cultures did, the case law guides us in applying the sixth commandment in other ways. Those who have swimming pools in their yards are advised (perhaps it's not too strong to say commanded) to put up a fence or some other barrier to prevent injury or drowning.

The point is that the moral law continues to the present day with little change, in contrast to the civil and ceremonial law. The Law expresses the will of God, which does not change in the sense that something that was once bad is now good. But times change, and Christians must discern the current application of the Law. The division of the law into three types—civil, ceremonial, and moral—

is not perfect, but it increases our understanding of the Law.

A word of caution: the ancient Hebrews did not recognize this three-part division of the Law. The moral, ceremonial, and civil laws were mixed together throughout the law codes. Nonetheless, as we look back on Law from the perspective of the New Testament, and especially as we reflect on how the Law continues into the present, the three categories are helpful, even though they do not answer all our questions.

Clearly, there are laws that we still observe, preeminently the Ten Commandments. That is, we *want* to observe them even if we often find ourselves falling short of them. To break any one law means breaking them all (James 2:10), so the law actually makes us guilty. How does Jesus relate to this Law we cannot keep perfectly? He is the only One who has kept it completely. He is the only One who has never sinned against God. And for that reason the Law drives us to Jesus Christ for forgiveness. He is the only One who can forgive the sins we commit against God.

Now that we are forgiven, we show our gratitude to Jesus by keeping His law. The Law is not given to initiate a relationship with God but to tell us how we can live a life that pleases Him. We obey the Law to thank God for what He has done for us. We still do it imperfectly, but nonetheless through His power we can now be obedient. By this, we imitate Jesus. We become more like Him in our thoughts, motives, and actions. As we live according to the principles of the Ten Commandments, we become more and more like the One whom we love—Jesus Christ.

FORMING A BIBLICAL WORLD VIEW

We are to think like Christ and obey Him in our actions. But, as we've said, becoming Christlike is not a magical transformation. It involves a process of growth resembling a seed that gradually blossoms into full maturity. And a critical aspect of that process is our formation of a worldview that reflects our Lord's will and character.

It's not easy to do.

Have you noticed the confusion that reigns today regarding worldviews and values? No single philosophy or world view dominates our own culture, not to speak of the cultures of the world. Globalization has brought different opinions into contact with one another, and, having no firm basis to begin with, our own Western culture suffers a crisis of belief. Our lack of confidence in absolutes has led to rampant relativism, resulting in loss of meaning. Viktor Frankl, the well-known psychotherapist and concentration camp survivor, captured the spirit and weakness of our age when he said, "Universal values are on the wane. That is why ever more people are caught in a feeling of aimlessness and emptiness."[2]

Even in the church, where the Bible remains at the center of our life together, confusion surfaces. We're all looking for some specific guidance to help us through life's decisions. Should I marry Ralph? Should I change careers? Should I go to class this morning or clean the house?

I remember with a twinge of embarrassment how, right after I became a Christian as a freshman in college, I used to look for daily guidance from the Lord by opening the Bible at random and pointing at a verse. Rarely did I find much help, no matter how much I tried to pull a secret meaning out of an obscure passage in Zephaniah. My intuition was correct in the sense that I believed the Bible to be the revelation of God's will for my life. But I misused God's gift by treating it as a magical talisman rather than taking the more difficult route of study and reflection that would help me develop a proper worldview.

Of course, we must not forget that Christianity makes a demand on our lives for obedience, and the Bible expresses to us by both example and imperative what form that obedience should take. Yet forming a biblical worldview requires going even deeper than the questions about specific do's and dont's. It means asking the most basic Big Questions about existence: Is there a purpose to life? Or do I simply live to survive the best I can, trying to eke out whatever pleasure makes life tolerable? Do my actions matter? Why should I care what happens to my neighbor, not to speak of some nameless refugee in some distant country?

One purpose of the Bible is to help us form a "proper"—as opposed to a "wrong"—worldview, one that is in keeping with the realities of the cosmos. Left to our own devices we would be completely misled; but God has graciously revealed Himself in the Bible, telling us who He is, who we are, and what our place is in His creation.

We are finite creatures, having only a minuscule understanding of the cosmos. Further, according to the Bible, we are sinners who have a tendency to distort what we do know. God, on the other hand, knows everything. The book of Job highlights the distance between God and you and me. Job 28 repeatedly asks the question, "Where can wisdom be found? Where does understanding dwell?" (12, 20). Through the words of Isaiah, God says:

"As the heavens are higher than the earth,
  so are my ways higher than your ways
  and my thoughts than your thoughts." (55:9)

Earlier Isaiah said, "Who has understood the mind of the LORD, or instructed him as his counselor?" (40:13). Paul knew that only one person really understood the mind of the Lord because He was the Son of the Father; that person is Jesus Christ. After quoting the Isaiah 40:13 passage, Paul went on to say to his Christian audience, "But we have the mind of Christ" (1 Corinthians 2:16). The context for this passage (2:6-16) speaks of Paul's message, which is a "message of wisdom" revealed by the Holy Spirit and understood by those who have the Holy Spirit. In a word, we gain the mind of Christ as we read the Bible prayerfully and with the Spirit's help.

Our worldview is formed by the Bible, then, but this doesn't happen automatically. We struggle with competing worldviews: "We take captive every thought to make it obedient to Christ" (2 Corinthians 10:5). Yet it's difficult to think like Christ because we live in a world that doesn't recognize His significance.

We grow up in an environment that acknowledges only the material aspects of the universe, denying the reality of the supernatural world that the Bible says surrounds us. We are trained by our culture to think like Elisha's servant who, when surrounded by a hostile army, saw only danger (2 Kings 6:8-23). Elisha had to pray that the man's eyesight be broadened. And when God responded to the prophet's prayer, the servant saw an incredible spiritual army surrounding the piddling army of the Arameans.

Elisha's prayer needs to be our prayer in our struggle to see the world the way it really is. History, theology, and ethics help. But so does poetry.

12

TAKE A
NEW LOOK

"Much is the force of heaven-bred poesy," said Shakespeare.

But to tell you the truth, I never much liked poetry. It seemed as if poets intended to confuse everyone, probably out of intellectual snobbery. Why didn't they just say, plainly and directly, what they wanted to say?

I remember reading the Bible as a young Christian. I had just given my life to Jesus in the summer between high school and college. I didn't have much experience as a Bible reader up to that point, but now I couldn't put the book down. As I read through its pages, I noticed many pages that looked like poetry. The poems were easy to spot because the lines were short, which meant there was a lot of white space on the pages.

This presence of large tracts of poetry in the Bible intrigued me. *Why would God inspire poets to communicate His word to us? Why subject us to poetry's difficulties and ambiguities?*

I couldn't answer my questions, but I dutifully read on, not always understanding what I was reading but making the attempt anyway. I think many thoughtful people have the same basic questions about biblical poetry: Why is there so much of it and how can I learn to read it profitably for spiritual growth?

LOOK AT HOW MUCH

It's mind-boggling to realize how much of the Bible, especially the Old Testament, comes to us in poetic form. Perhaps the largest amount of poetry is found in the longest book of the Bible, the Psalms. Here we have one hundred fifty separate poems, constituting a book that functioned as the hymnbook of the Old Testament people of God. And the Wisdom books also are predominately poetic — Proverbs, Job, Song of Songs, and Ecclesiastes.[1] Read through any of these books and see how well the form of poetry conveys an emotional message that is best spoken directly to the soul.

More fascinating are the prophets. Most of the prophets communicated to their audience using poetic forms. God sent the prophets to speak to the people about their sins. Their mission was to get the people of Israel back on course in their relationship with God. These counter-cultural "trouble-makers" often crashed into the scene with a harsh message of divine judgment. Why was that message best communicated in poetic form? For one thing, we know that their words needed to make heavy impact. "God needs prophets in order to make Himself known, and all prophets are necessarily artists. What a prophet has to say can never be said in prose."[2] Poetry suited the unique mission of these spokesmen for God because it cut to the quick with piercing efficiency.

Even the history and law books of the Old Testament contain poems. Think of the blessings and curses of Jacob (Genesis 49) and Moses (Deuteronomy 33). In addition, these books contain songs of military celebration (Exodus 15, Judges 5). There's even one book comprised of a song that laments the defeat of Judah at the hands of the Babylonians (the book of Lamentations). These portions of history and law could hardly be communicated with the same power and depth of emotion if they were expressed in prose alone.

While the biggest portion of poetry is in the Old Testament, we also discover poems in the New Testament, which appear at critical junctures of the text. A short list would include Mary's Magnificat

(Luke 1:46-55), Zechariah's song (Luke 1:68-79), and Paul's meditation on the power and humility of Christ (Philippians 2:6-11). Clearly, the sheer bulk of poetic material in the Bible is staggering. If collected in one place, it would be longer than the entire New Testament. But it's all there because of its unique power to reach deep into our souls and move us in a way that largely bypasses the rational and speaks directly to our hearts. Yet to apply this important part of the Bible to our lives does require some intellectual effort. We must, at the very least, arrive at a basic strategy for interpreting it.

LEARN TO READ IT RIGHT

The trick is to learn how to read poetry in a way that respects its original, heart-targeted intention without doing so much analysis that we suck the life out of it. It's tempting to just read and allow ourselves to be carried away. However, the poets of Israel, inspired by God, followed a set pattern of poetry writing that is somewhat foreign to us. We can read this kind of literature with richer reward if we recapture the conventions of Hebrew poetry writing. Consider these three key elements:

Conciseness. Any poetry is quite different from ordinary speech. When we talk with each other, we often repeat ourselves to make our message understood. We stop in mid-sentence and start again. We stray from the topic and then wander back. And we're fairly unreflective about how we say something—usually we just let our words flow.

Poets, on the other hand, are intensely self-conscious about how they say something, and poetry prides itself on its compact language. Poets say a lot using just few words. They pack the greatest meaning into every word and phrase. Read just the first verse of the famous poem, Psalm 23:

The LORD is my shepherd, I shall not be in want.

In its original Hebrew form, this couplet contains only four words! To realize the power of these few words, write out in prose your understanding of what it says and means. No doubt, you'll use a number of sentences and still won't exhaust the meaning. Your prose paraphrase will have to include a description of how the shepherd image affects your feelings. The picture of God as a shepherd communicates a warmth about God that can't be captured by a mere prose description of Him as a supernatural being who protects, guides, and cares.

How do the poets achieve their conciseness? First, biblical poetry plays down the use of conjunctions. Conjunctions are usually short words ("but," "and," "therefore," "however"), but they give explicit guidance for relating concepts in a sentence or paragraph. Since there are no conjunctions in the Hebrew of Psalm 23:1, we have to supply them. We usually understand the relationship this way: "(Since) the LORD is my shepherd, (therefore) I shall not be in want."

A second reason poetry is so compact is that it frequently uses imagery. Images catch our attention because of the dissimilarity between the "real" object being described and the image connected to it. Yet in its concise application of image to reality, poetry helps us reflect on how the two things are alike.

Since the poetry of the Bible is concise, compressed language, it requires a different pace of reading. We need to slow down and carefully meditate on it. This sounds simple, but we're so busy we rarely do it. We rush through our devotional times, thinking it more admirable to read a lot more of the Bible than a little bit. The poetry of the Bible calls us to slow down and be present to God's gentle way of teaching us. As poet Alexander Pope once said: "Some people never learn anything because they understand everything too soon."

Parallelism. Here is the key to unlocking the depth of expression in Hebrew poetry—understanding its parallel structures. Consider this example:

Why do the nations conspire
    and the peoples plot in vain?
The kings of the earth take their stand
    and the rulers gather together
against the LORD
    and against his Anointed One.
"Let us break their chains," they say,
    "and throw off their fetters." (Psalm 2:1-3)

When I first started reading the Psalms, I wondered about all the repetition. Sometimes it seemed that the poet just kept repeating himself for no apparent reason. Why all this echoing? I soon found myself reading quickly over such poetry thinking that once was enough. As it turned out, I seriously misunderstood an important characteristic of Hebrew poetry, a quality that, once understood, would lead me into a much more satisfying experience with Scripture.

This characteristic goes by the rather dry name "parallelism" and is the most obvious trait of Old Testament poetry. It describes the large amount of repetition between lines and parts of lines. In the past, parallelism was taken as a simple literary ornament. That is, the two repeating versets say the same thing; the poet simply used two different sets of words. And we do get some artistic satisfaction out of that. Yet close study of poems in the Bible shows that this approach is too superficial. The second part of the line always in some sense advances the thought of the first part:

> Blessed is the man
> > who does not walk in the counsel of the wicked
> or stand in the way of sinners
> > or sit in the seat of mockers.

In Psalm 1:1 we actually have a three-part parallelism. As we study this verse, we notice similarities in the parallel phrases, especially a similarity of theme (the description of a wise man's attitude toward evil). But notice also a progression and intensification of the main thought. Look at the verbs: *walk, stand,* and *sit.* In the development of the metaphor of the righteous man, his connection with evil is more and more strongly denied. As we move from walk to sit, we are progressing from a casual acquaintance with evil to a settled one.

As we read biblical poetry, we must always meditate carefully on the relationship between the versets and the lines. This relationship takes many forms, from nearly synonymous meaning to an almost totally different meaning. Once again, this gives us a reason to *slow down* and *meditate* when we read poetry.

Imagery. While we find imagery in all types of literature, it washes over us in waves when we read poems. How do we tell when something is an image, and how do we interpret the image once we recognize it?

An image is usually based on a comparison. The writer associates two different things in order to throw a new perspective on one of them. We use images this way all the time in everyday speech. When someone repeatedly knocks things down and breaks them, we say, "He's as clumsy as a bull in a china shop!" In this rather simple image, we compare a person with an animal. We equate two things that are fundamentally dissimilar but that share some key traits.

Remember your English class? You studied two major categories of images based on comparison: metaphors and similes. Similes are obvious comparisons because they usually use the words *like* or *as.*

The image in the previous paragraph is a simile. A metaphor, however, brings two fundamentally different things into direct relationship with each other by saying it without using *like* or *as*: "the city was a gleaming jewel"; "his muscles, cords of twisted steel, bulged from his shirt." Being so direct, metaphors are often more striking (or even shocking) than similes. "John is as noble as a lion" might be literally true, while "John is a lion" would never be true. Yet the metaphor does, in the proper context, communicate the same truth as the simile.

The Bible abounds in images conveyed by simile and metaphor. Look at some of the descriptions of God, for instance: He is a rock, a fortress, a warrior, a shepherd, and on and on. Other images occur as well: Nineveh is a lion and a harlot (Nahum 2:12–3:4); evil is a beast (Revelation 13).

How do we distinguish an image from literal language? Similes are easy to recognize because of *like* or *as*. But it's sometimes difficult to identify a metaphor. A rule of thumb is to realize that we are dealing with a metaphor whenever it would become ridiculous or absurd to interpret the connection literally. This approach allows for many gray edges. What one person thinks is ridiculous may not be so strange to another. Also, some metaphorical language is subtle or falls into the category of "dead" or "frozen" metaphor (for instance, when we refer to the "leg" of a table).[3]

Metaphors are usually easy to recognize in context because of the striking dissimilarities in the two things being compared.

> The Lord awoke as from sleep,
> as a man wakes from the stupor of wine. (Psalm 78:65)

The comparison between the Lord God of the universe and a man waking out of a drunken sleep is striking, even shocking. No one would fail to recognize this as a simile. Indeed, images usually grab our attention by presenting such wild comparisons. Of course, it is not the purpose of the image to describe God as a drunk. After it has gotten our attention and led us into reflection, we realize that the image means that God has become active again for His people after a lengthy period of silence and apparent absence.

How do we interpret an image? Once again, we must slow down and meditate. Once we focus our attention on the image we must ask ourselves in what ways these two things are alike and in what ways they are not. Psalm 131:2 presents an image of God as a mother and our soul as a weaned child:

> But I have stilled and quieted my soul;
>> like a weaned child with its mother,
>> like a weaned child is my soul within me.

This image has two points of comparison. In the first place, God is like a mother. Now that we've recognized this comparison, we need to ask the point. God is like a mother in that He displays compassion toward His people. Feminine images surface elsewhere when biblical writers speak of God's mercy (see Isaiah 66:13), and indeed the Hebrew word for *compassion* is the same as the word for "womb."

But notice the second part of the comparison. Our soul is like a weaned child. We have to ask ourselves why the psalmist used "weaned" because this precise term is unnecessary to the main point that established God's compassionate nature. As we visualize the image, we realize that unweaned children are anything but calm and peaceful on their mothers' laps. They squirm and fidget—wanting to get at the milk! But a weaned child quietly rests in the mother's protective embrace.

While conciseness, parallelism, and imagery are the three most common features of poetry in the Bible, the poet had a host of other "tricks of the trade" at his disposal. For instance, the poet occasionally structured his work using the Hebrew alphabet as an acrostic. Even English translations of Psalm 119 reveal this feature of the psalm, but other poems also display this feature in the Hebrew without the English translations conveying it.

We won't go into detail about acrostics or describe other poetic devices in the Bible at this point.[4] Just keep in mind that a careful reader will begin to note recurrent devices in the poems of the Old and New Testaments—poetic devices that enhance the meaning.

LET YOURSELF PARTICIPATE

The meaning we receive from the Bible's poetry is the result of our decision to participate in it wholeheartedly. I encourage you to receive its artistry as a wonderful gift of God to you. If your heart is open, you will find it to be an enthralling conveyor of the transcendent. In a sense, we could say that poetry, because it uses words as its medium, is the essence of creativity, for creation itself sprang from words: "And God said . . ."

And it was so!

Amazingly, God invites us to participate with Him in His matchless words. I'll conclude by letting Eugene Petersen, author of *Living the*

Message, tell us why we ought never casually skim over such magnificent language:

> Poetry is essential . . . because poetry is original speech. The word is creative: it brings into being what was not there before—perception, relationship, belief. Out of the silent abyss a sound is formed: people hear what was not heard before and are changed by the sound from loneliness into love. Out of the blank abyss a picture is formed by means of metaphor: people see what they did not see before and are changed by the image from anonymity into love. Words create. God's word creates; our words can participate in the creation.[5]

13

LANGUAGE OF THE HEART

As a young Christian, I thought that the one and only purpose of the Bible was to inform my intellect about God. I thought that becoming a Christian was primarily an intellectual decision—a reasoned analysis of the world's many philosophies and religious systems that resulted in choosing Christianity as the correct approach. The Bible's purpose, then, was to present the intellectual case for Christianity.

Not only was my view of the Bible naive, so was my understanding of who I am as a human being before God. I am more than a mind God wants to claim. He desires my whole being—body, mind, emotions, imagination, and will. This wholeness defines all of us as spiritual people, and God wants the whole of us to know Him and to love Him.

COMMUNICATING THE EXTRAORDINARY

God inspired poetry toward that purpose. It does inform our intellect, of course. After all, the poets tell us who God is and who we are. But the Psalms also arouse our emotions, stimulate our imaginations, and appeal to our wills by giving us wonderful literary paintings of the nature of God. He is a king, rock, shepherd, and warrior. The Song of Songs addresses us as God's creatures, helping us to understand the wonders of our sexuality. All of this is done through a language that goes beyond the merely intellectual to communicate the extraordinary.

Of course, we must be quick to point out that the prose narratives or stories of the Bible are written in such a way that they, too, go beyond simply giving us information. But the poetry of the Bible more obviously addresses the nonrational parts of our being.

Try a simple test. Before you read on here, stop and read Exodus 14. This chapter recounts the crossing of the Red Sea. It is more than factual. We can sense the anger of the Egyptians and the fear of the Israelites. And we feel awe at God's display of cataclysmic power. Now read on in Exodus 15 . . .

> I will sing to the LORD,
>   for He is highly exalted.
> The horse and its rider
>   He has hurled into the sea.
> The LORD is my strength and my song;
>   He has become my salvation.
> He is my God, and I will praise him,
>   my father's God, and I will exalt him.
> The LORD is a warrior;
>   the LORD is his name.
> Pharaoh's chariots and his army
>   He has hurled into the sea.
> The best of Pharaoh's officers
>   are drowned in the Red Sea.
> The deep waters have covered them;
>   they sank to the depths like a stone. (Exodus 15:1-5)

We are immediately swept into the moment, learning about what God did at the Red Sea. But feel the emotion! The image of God as a warrior invites us to experience God's protection and care for us as His people, even today. We, too, want to sing out in praise.

Yet most of the time we live by routine. We get up in the morning, brush our teeth, get dressed, kiss our spouses and kids good-bye, and then drive off to work. After work we come home, eat dinner, do some chores, maybe read a book or watch TV, and head off to sleep, only to begin again the next day. Many of our tasks seem never ending. My wife likens doing the laundry for her family of five to the Myth of Sisyphus. In that story, Sisyphus is condemned to pushing a large circular rock to the top of a mountain every morning, only to have it roll immediately to the bottom so that he can begin once again the next morning—with the routine pushing.

Occasionally we're lifted out of the mundane, though, and get a glimpse of something larger. I may take a break from doing the bills, another Sisyphus-like task, to go over to my wife and give her a kiss, and soon we're in another realm. Love can inspire us and lift our spirits beyond the present and the urgent. *And poetry is the language of love.* It is a way of communicating that is out of the ordinary. It is rhythmic and bursting with emotion. Poetry ornaments the present with imagery, showing not only what is, but what is possible. It breaks through the routine and lifts us out of the mundane . . . into the presence of God.

Consider the poetry in the Song of Songs, for example. The lover and the beloved embrace and are swept away in a sea of emotion. Their descriptions of each other (4:1-5:1, 10-16) are not precise and realistic; rather, they drip with desire and anticipation.

Or look into the book of Hosea. Here God turns to His adulterous people, and we can almost see the tears in His eyes when He speaks as the Poet to them of His enduring patience:

> How can I give you up, Ephraim?
> > How can I hand you over, Israel?
> How can I treat you like Admah?
> > How can I make you like Zeboiim?
> My heart is changed within me;
> > all my compassion is aroused.
> I will not carry out my fierce anger,

> nor will I turn and devastate Ephraim.
> For I am God, and not man—
>   the Holy One among you.
>   I will not come in wrath. (Hosea 11:8-9)

Biblical poetry is the language of God's love for us. And it is also the language of our love for Him—the language of worship.

WORSHIPING WITH OUR WHOLE BEING

We owe God everything—the very air we breathe, our good relationships, our joy, our achievements, our material blessings. All are God's gifts to us. We deserve none of them. Above any of these things, we should be thankful for our relationship with Him. We have offended God greatly, but He not only has entered into a relationship with us, He sent his own Son to die on a cross for our sins.

When we realize these great and wonderful truths, we are moved to an almost inarticulate gratitude. We don't know what to say because mere words seem inadequate. Poetry takes us out of the mundane and helps us see God as being right with us, while giving us words that are fitting to express the emotion we feel. This is true, even when we are moved to worship while profound questions continue to rage within us.

> Sometimes God answers us with questions—questions
> that leave us humbled, awed, speechless, weak and
> believing—believing not because we've found the
> answer, but because we've seen God. It doesn't matter
> that we have more questions now than when we
> started. It matters that we see God, for in the seeing,
> we discover that the truest answer to all our questions
> is to worship him.[1]

The biblical poetry helps us worship at some deep level within us, even when our intellects can only go so far along the path with our spirits. In this way, our love for God can continue, strong and vibrant, in spite of intellectual doubt or even emotional despair. How often this comes through in the book of Psalms! It is not surprising that the most important book of worship in the Bible, the Psalms, is a poetic book. The Psalms show the close connection between poem and song. They are the hymn book of the Bible and give us words to address this powerful and compassionate Being who has so graced our lives.

> O LORD, our Lord,
>   how majestic is your name in all the earth! (Psalm 8:1)

The Psalms turn us to God when trouble comes (see Psalm 69), even when that trouble comes ultimately from Him. In the latter case, the psalmist displays an honesty that is the product of intimate relationship.

> Has God forgotten to be merciful?
>   Has he in anger withheld his compassion?
>   (Psalm 77:9)

Poetry is the language of worship, of intimate, emotionally intense communication with God. It is a language that properly lifts us out of the mundane to the heights with God. What impact are you letting it have on you, personally? One secular writer explained poetry's effect this way:

> Experience has taught me, when I am shaving of a
> morning, to keep watch over my thoughts, because,
> if a line of poetry strays into my memory, my skin
> bristles so that the razor ceases to act. The seat of
> this sensation is the pit of the stomach.[2]

When has the Bible touched you—your skin, your stomach—this way? If the power of merely human words can have such a striking effect, then what might the power of Spirit-inspired biblical poetry do within us? After all, the Lord is the Poet of all poets.

SINGING WITH THE POET JESUS

The Psalms present poetry to address our Maker and Savior. These poems and songs may also be described as prayers because they form an intimate dialogue between us and God. In a truly mysterious way God uses these human voices that have been addressed to Him in order to speak to us.

As we continue to read in the Bible, we see other places where God communicates with us as a Poet. For instance, He tells us the story of Job and his friends in poetic form. The poetry of this book lifts up a particular historical moment and raises it to a universal principle. Job's poetic form invites us to consider for our own lives the implications of this man's struggle with undeserved suffering. We can't read the book of Job and automatically assume that we suffer because of our sin. God in His wisdom often hides from us the ultimate purpose of our suffering. As with Job, He requires not our understanding but our surrender to Him.

The poetry of the prophets presents God's emotional speeches of love, but it also presents His disappointment, anger, and judgment. Our whole being is addressed by these hard-hitting poetical speeches.

God as poet teaches us something about His character by His choice to speak to us in this artful way. We learn that God is interested in our emotions and in beauty, as well as in our minds and our intellect. Because God wants us to "know" Him we may think that emotions and beauty would distract us. Beauty, we may think, is deceptive. It hides what's important and true. But God knows better. It's not a matter of truth *or* beauty; *both* reflect God's glorious presence. This realization should inspire us to seek not only what is right but also what is lovely in our lives.

God pursues beauty and sings songs to His people. Why then should we be surprised to turn to the New Testament and discover that His Son is a poet as well? Time and again Jesus speaks the words of the poet to articulate His heart. When He confronted those who accepted neither John the Baptist's call to repentance nor His own to forgiveness and joy, He uttered a threatening poem:

> "We played the flute for you,
>   and you did not dance;
> we sang a dirge,
>   and you did not mourn." (Matthew 11:17)

When Jesus taught, He taught in parables, a highly artistic art form filled with imagery from real life. But to hear the most poignant of all His words, we must turn to the moment that won our salvation when He hung on the cross. At that critical moment, how did He give voice to his suffering? He cried out in the song of the ancient poet, "My God, my God, why have you forsaken me?" (Matthew 27:46, quoting Psalm 22:1).

The author of the book of Hebrews tells us that Jesus doesn't sing alone; He sings with us. Jesus is our brother who tells us,

> "I will declare your name to my brothers;
>> in the presence of the congregation I will sing
>> your praises." (Hebrews 2:12)

READING POETRY FOR SPIRITUAL GROWTH

As you read the poetry of the Bible, keep in mind a few key principles: first, remember that the poet says much while using few words. He has carefully structured his poem, so slow down and spend time looking for the relationship between versets, lines, and even stanzas. Especially reflect on the relationship between versets that make up a parallel line. How do the subsequent versets expand the thought of the first one?

Next, identify and unpack the imagery. What is being compared and what are the similarities? What does the poet intend to teach by using the image?

Then look for other poetic devices. Some, such as acrostics, will be obvious. Others, such as Hebrew sound plays, will escape the reader of the English version of the Bible. Consult the best commentaries to discover what is taking place in the original language. Then reflect not only on what you are learning from the poem, but how the poem arouses your emotions, stimulates your imagination, and appeals to your will.

Finally, think of God as the Poet of the poem. Think of Jesus singing the song with you. What insight does that give you into the character of God?

14

THE SUPREME GOAL

B ill looked at the kitchen clock as he quietly entered from the garage—almost midnight, but it had been worth it. He had worked all day at the office and then had dinner with the representatives of ICB, Inc. They had been intrigued by his earlier presentation, and he knew he had the right figures to close the deal.

After dinner, they'd sat down for the negotiations, which lasted until 10:30 P.M., and then it had taken an hour to drive home. He knew Susan wasn't pleased that he'd missed another one of Heather's softball games, but he'd make it up to her somehow, and soon. Susan needed to realize that if she wanted the BMW and the membership at the club, he would have to work very hard to pay for it. And Heather loved to shop from the catalogues.

145

> The LORD does not let the righteous go hungry
>> but he thwarts the craving of the wicked.
> (Proverbs 10:3)

Ten o'clock already! Amanda uttered an expletive under her breath and then said to Angela, her roommate, "I missed my nine o'clock class again. Why do they have to make classes so early?"

"If you didn't party half the night, you might be able to rouse yourself for class," said Angela, who had returned from her eight o'clock class and was studying at her desk.

"Well, that's fine, but what if I flunk Literary Criticism!"

"You won't; the teacher's in love with you. He'd give you a passing grade even if you didn't write the paper."

Amanda let out another expletive. "The paper . . . when is it due?"

"End of the week, airhead. Maybe you should just go home and ask your father for a down payment on your eventual inheritance. You won't have to work a day in your life anyway."

"I know, but for some weird reason, my parents want me to do this college thing."

"Some people have it made," Angela muttered, as she turned back to her economics textbook.

> Do not love sleep or you will grow poor;
>> stay awake and you will have food to spare.
> (Proverbs 20:13)

"God is good," Robert whispered in his wife's ear as they hugged. They stood in the middle of the living room surrounded by friends and relatives who had just greeted him with a loud "Surprise!"

The occasion: his promotion to full partner in his firm. It had been a long haul, beginning in inner-city Detroit. He'd had no father to guide or nurture him, and school was a daily horror. But he'd kept at it, and away from other distractions and temptations, in spite of occasional threats from a few classmates.

He did well enough in high school to land a scholarship at a fairly decent university, and it was there he really devoted himself to hard work. He graduated summa cum laude and ended up in a prestigious law school where he worked long, grueling hours.

Then he entered the firm. They were glad to have a minority face in the office, but for the senior partners it was just window dressing.

He'd had to work harder than anyone to come to this moment. He had won their support by his God-given talent and long hours.

His wife, Karen, was an incredible support. She had worked to keep them financially afloat and now had a budding career of her own. She worked hard, too, and devoted so much time to their two wonderful little girls. God is indeed good, Robert thought to himself again, as he enjoyed an evening celebrating the capstone of many years of hard work.

> The blessing of the LORD brings wealth,
> and he adds no trouble to it. (Proverbs 10:22)

Do you recognize any of these folks? Each of them is living life the best they know how. Some are smarter than others. Some have Christ in their lives, and some don't give "religion" a second thought. Some come from dysfunctional family backgrounds, some have helpful friends, some have strong willpower, others feel helpless most of the time.

Maybe you see yourself here—at least you see a neighbor or two. But in whatever way you connect with their situations, the common factor in their lives and yours is the need for wisdom. Without sizable amounts of wisdom, none of us can live a satisfying life. We need it like the air we breathe.

WHAT DOES IT MEAN TO BE WISE?

Rarely do we call anyone "wise" today. Bright, quick, intelligent, even shrewd, but never wise. When we think of someone who is wise, we conjure a picture of an old person dressed in a robe, sitting serenely in the lotus position uttering words of incredible insight. Today we prize intelligence and action over wisdom.

Recent studies, though, have questioned the value of raw intelligence.[1] It's simply not true that people with high IQs live better, more successful, and happier lives than those who aren't so "bright." Straight A's don't necessarily transform into great careers and certainly do not assure excellent marriages or relationships.

The Bible doesn't put down intelligence, but it never prizes the accumulation of knowledge above all. It speaks of wisdom as the highest goal.

> Wisdom is supreme; therefore get wisdom.
> Though it cost all you have, get understanding. (Proverbs 4:7)

> For wisdom is more precious than rubies,
>> and nothing you desire can compare with her.
>> (Proverbs 8:11)

Not intelligence, but wisdom is what the Bible holds out to us as a supreme goal in life. What is this wisdom that has such incredible value? Wisdom, in the Bible, describes "the skill of living." The English word gives us an insight into the Hebrew concept. The word is formed from two parts: *wis*, which means "wise-knowing," and *dom*, which means "dominion." Wisdom refers, then, to "the realm of the knowing one."

Christian wisdom illuminates our experience. It interprets our experiences, not from our earthbound perspective but from a divine perspective. Even the author of Ecclesiastes, the least enthusiastic of all wisdom teachers, affirms this when he says,

> I saw that wisdom is better than folly,
>> just as light is better than darkness.
> The wise man has eyes in his head,
>> while the fool walks in the darkness.
>> (Ecclesiastes 2:13-14)

The teaching of the Bible is that a wise person knows how to act and how to speak in appropriate ways that enrich life. Yet we can't achieve wisdom by learning a list of rules and regulations that work in each and every circumstance of life. The wisdom of the Bible presents *principles* of godly living and advocates a mindset from which we can apply them. It takes a wise person to know how to apply the principles. The wisdom teachers of ancient Israel felt great satisfaction when they spoke the right word at the right time:

> A man finds joy in giving an apt reply—
>> and how good is a timely word! (Proverbs 15:23)

The book of Proverbs recognizes that its sayings can be horribly misused. If a fool, as compared to a wise man or woman, tries to apply a proverb, the results will be ineffective and could be disastrous.

> Like a lame man's legs that hang limp
>> is a proverb in the mouth of a fool. . . .
> Like a thornbush in a drunkard's hand
>> is a proverb in the mouth of a fool. (Proverbs 26:7,9)

This underscores a very important distinction when we read the wisdom literature. What we discover are not laws or promises; they are general principles of godly living.

LIVING BY THE PRINCIPLES

In the vignettes at the beginning of this chapter, we saw Robert working hard and being rewarded with success. This confirms a principle stated in the Proverbs. We can tell from life experience that this is the way the world usually operates: no pain, no gain. We work hard to achieve success.

However, that isn't the way it always happens. The book of Proverbs says that laziness leads to poverty. But sometimes there are mitigating circumstances. Some people have rich parents who cater to them, as in the case of Amanda.

Then there's Bill. He works hard and has achieved success. He could quote the Proverbs to justify his lifestyle. However, his workaholism is killing his family. Even though he's fulfilled the proverbial formula regarding work, could we really call him—in the words of the book of Proverbs—a "righteous man"?

When my mother and aunt used to offer to help my grandmother cook the turkey for Thanksgiving, she would shoo them away by saying, "Too many cooks spoil the broth!" We grandchildren were glad for that, since my grandmother was an exceptional cook. But after the meal, when we all felt like collapsing on the floor in front of the television, she would turn to us with dish towel in hand and say, "Many hands make light work!"

All proverbs, whether they're from the Bible or not, are like a heat-seeking missile heading straight toward the target of right living. It's part of what makes a proverb a proverb. However, the biblical Proverbs were never meant to be applied in a mechanistic way. Unfortunately, from ancient to modern times people have used them in precisely this manner.

Think of the three friends of Job—Eliphaz, Bildad, and Zophar. They all sang a similar song: Job suffered because of his sin. The wicked suffer; the righteous are blessed with success. If Job suffered, he must be a sinner!

Yet the book of Job is quite clear that the friends were wrong. We never really learn why Job suffered, but we're informed that his sin had nothing to do with it. The three friends belied their claim to be wise with such an incredible misinterpretation of the situation.

The book of Proverbs makes it quite obvious that its teachings are not laws or unalterable regulations. They are time-sensitive principles of living that can be applied to a variety of circumstances. One way the book shows this is by having certain proverbs teach the opposite of others. And in one case, such apparently conflicting words of wisdom rub up against one another in the text:

> Do not answer a fool according to his folly,
>> or you will be like him yourself.
> Answer a fool according to his folly,
>> or he will be wise in his own eyes. (Proverbs 26:4-5)

The wise person here is given guidance—not an iron-clad law—about interacting with a fool. As he engages in conversation with someone who acts foolishly, he must then make a decision: Do I answer him or do I ignore what he's saying? In other words, the wise person must judge what kind of fool he's dealing with. Is this the type of person who will grow proud and more confident of himself if left unanswered, or is this the type of person who will drag me into an unending and profitless argument? The answer to this question will determine how one acts in the presence of a fool.

Once again, the Proverbs are true, all things being equal.

But they must be properly applied. Consider how much pain has been introduced into the lives of godly parents by people who hammer them with the following proverb after their adult children go astray:

> Train a child in the way he should go,
>> and when he is old he will not turn from it.
>> (Proverbs 22:6)

Those who hold up this proverb to grieving parents—telling them they did a poor job raising their son or daughter—are like Job's friends. A husband, for instance, could berate his wife, telling her she's responsible for their children's difficulties because of the way she catered to them when they were young.

No, wisdom comes not from laws but from abiding by time-sensitive principles. Yet this doesn't lessen wisdom's importance as we try to make our way through a difficult world. The purpose of biblical wisdom is to give us principles for living *and* to form our minds so that we might be wise in the application of those principles.

All of this is to say that wisdom-seeking ought to be an abiding quest in our lives. It can be our daily prayer as we approach the Lord each new morning. If you'd like more wisdom in your days, why not try repeating this classic prayer as you arise, starting tomorrow? And then look into the book of Proverbs for spiritual refreshment.

> O Lord, thou greatest and most true Light,
> whence the light of the day doth spring!
> O Light, which dost lighten every man
> that cometh into the world!
> O thou Wisdom of the eternal Father,
> lighten my mind, that I may see
> only those things that please thee,
> and may be blinded to all other things.
> Grant that I may walk in thy ways,
> and that nothing else
> may be light and pleasant. Amen.
> John Bradford, A.D. 1510-1555

15

FIND IT...
WHERE?

H e sits on an ash heap and moans. With his family and livelihood wiped out, he's left with nothing—except intense physical pain.

Three of his friends come to "comfort" him. They have insight into his predicament, as well as a solution to offer. Automatically categorizing him as a great sinner, they give him the answer to his problem—repent!

But the man knows he hasn't been disobedient, so he feels he shouldn't be suffering. And he wants to call God on the carpet, tell God that he's been treated unjustly. In a temporary moment of insight, he has a glimpse of the truth when he raises the profound question, "Where can wisdom be found?"

SEARCHING OUT GOD'S WISDOM
When the suffering Job asked his critical question,[1] he understood that wisdom is even more inaccessible to

humanity than the precious metals and jewels dug with great effort from the depths of the earth. Finally he admits that wisdom can be found in only one place.

> Where then does wisdom come from?
> Where does understanding dwell?
> It is hidden from the eyes of every living thing,
> concealed even from the birds of the air.
> Destruction and Death say,
> "Only a rumor of it has reached our ears."
> God understands the way to it
> and he alone knows where it dwells,
> for he views the ends of the earth
> and sees everything under the heavens.
> (Job 28:20-24)

Wisdom is found in God.

God gives us His insight through the Scriptures. The pursuit of wisdom is an important theme throughout the Bible, but only a handful of books—Job, Ecclesiastes, Proverbs—focus on the subject.

The most obvious collection of wisdom is the book of Proverbs. It's a collection of wise sayings, some fairly long (see Proverbs 1-9,31), and some the typically short statements we commonly label proverbial (see chapters 10–30). These wisdom teachings probably come from different time periods, but the majority were written and/or collected by Solomon, the most well-known wise man in Israel's history (1 Kings 4:29-34).

Job and Ecclesiastes are also wisdom books. They have a different form and a different tone than Proverbs, but they address the wisdom theme as well. We can see how the book of Job is a narrative guard against reading the optimistic principles of Proverbs too mechanically. Good people do suffer, and bad people do prosper— at least for a while.

Ecclesiastes, too, is a wisdom book that makes sure we don't approach life in a simplistic way. Many readers of Ecclesiastes fail to recognize there are two voices in the book. *Qohelet*, the Hebrew name for the one often called the Preacher or Teacher, does most of the talking (1:12–12:7). His voice sounds a rather depressing note throughout. Anyone who's read the book knows what I mean. The refrains hammer at us: "Everything is meaningless"; life is just so much "chasing the wind." The Teacher continually asks the question, "What profit is there?" with the assumed answer that there is none.

Qohelet searches for meaning in many areas of life—wisdom, folly, pleasure, work, relationships. But just when he seems to find something significant, he remembers that he will die. Since he believed that nothing survived death, he felt that death rendered every status and achievement null and void.

But there's a second voice in Ecclesiastes, the voice that brings the book to conclusion (12:8-14). Qohelet had restricted his vision to "under the sun," that is, he viewed life apart from the reality and revelation of God. From our standpoint, what he's describing is the world feeling the effects of the Fall (see Romans 8:18-27 for a description of those effects). The concluding voice warns us of the danger of thinking about life apart from God and then uses it to drive us right back to God. The book ends this way:

> Now all has been heard;
>> here is the conclusion of the matter:
> Fear God and keep his commandments,
>> for this is the whole 'duty' of man.
> For God will bring every deed into judgment,
>> including every hidden thing,
>> whether it is good or evil. (Ecclesiastes 12:13-14)

All three of these books, in their different ways, show us the value of true wisdom. It isn't something learned primarily from others or gleaned only from observing the world, for Qohelet's mere observation of life led him to the conclusion that it was all "meaningless." The true wisdom that gives significance to our lives comes from God. The last verses of Ecclesiastes turn us to God and tell us to fear Him. This phrase reminds us of the first verses of Proverbs (1:1-7), which introduce the whole book and conclude with the statement, "The fear of the LORD is the beginning of knowledge."

A WISE VIEW OF THE WORLD

True human wisdom, then, begins with an attitude of submission to God. Since the Bible is God's Word to us, we can see that the wise person submits to the insight and instruction of the Bible. But let's be more specific. What are the crucial attitudes we'll have to display if we're to enjoy a life shaped by biblical wisdom? Consider these three:

An approach of respectful fear. Those who are wise fear the Lord. This attitude radically affects how a person sees the world.

> The fear of the Lord—that is wisdom,
> and to shun evil is understanding. (Job 28:28)

But what does the phrase, "the fear of the Lord" mean? Some people emaciate the truth by insisting the word doesn't really mean "fear"; it means to "hold in awe" or "revere." After all, the thinking goes, God—to whom we have continuous access—is our best friend. Jesus is a "friend of sinners." Therefore, there's no need to be afraid of our good buddy God.

To focus exclusively on these truths about God robs us of the comfort of knowing that God is also the Creator—the One who sustains the entire universe, the Judge who determines who lives and who dies, who goes to heaven and who goes to hell. He is a being so far above our thoughts that we can't even fathom Him.

Our rather sappy, sentimental Christianity muffles the power behind Jesus' words: "I tell you, my friends, do not be afraid of those who kill the body and after that can do no more. But I will show you whom you should fear: Fear him who, after the killing of the body, has power to throw you into hell. Yes, I tell you, fear him" (Luke 12:4-5).

To fear God is to know that a moment of existence without Him is hell. We can live in various degrees of distance from Him—each step a foot closer to the dark hollow of Hades. We are to fear the loss of existence; we are to fear the loss of the very essence of humanness as we walk on the edge of rebellion.

To fear God is to look at the world from God's perspective. This radically changes our view of everything. Indeed, if we fear God, we will have a different view of the things that strike fear into our hearts right now. Notice how God speaks to Isaiah's generation. They fear other things because they do not have the fear of God:

> "Whom have you so dreaded and feared
>   that you have been false to me,
> and have neither remembered me
>   nor pondered this in your hearts?
> Is it not because I have long been silent
>   that you do not fear me?" (Isaiah 57:11)

In God's presence, all human fears disappear like smoke dispersed by the wind. The fear of God overwhelms the fear of the world.

A willingness to pursue. Proverbs presents us with an intriguing picture of the pursuit of wisdom. To understand its intention, we have to suspend our modern sensibilities for a moment and realize that the book is addressed primarily to the *men* of Israel. The men of the nation were to assimilate the message and then teach it to their children and wives.

Proverbs is a fascinating book. The first nine chapters present you and me, the reader in the story, as a character. We readers are the young men addressed by our parents and told to pursue one woman and one woman only, whose name is Wisdom. Further, our parents warn us that as we walk the path of life we will be tempted to go after other women, particularly one named Folly.

This teaching comes to a climax in Proverbs 9, just before we begin the short, pithy aphorisms. In chapter 9, we, the readers, are walking along the path of life. Suddenly we hear a voice calling to us:

> Let all who are simple come in here!
> Come, eat my food
> and drink the wine I have mixed.
> Leave your simple ways and you will live;
> walk in the way of understanding. (Proverbs 9:4-6)

We look in the direction of the voice and see the figure of a beautiful woman standing before her magnificent house. Her house sits on the top of a hill, prominently displayed. The smells of her delicious meals reach us and we feel ourselves drawn to her. She wants us to come to her, dine with her, become intimate with her.

We feel ourselves moving in her direction, but suddenly we hear a second voice, sweetly calling us from the other side of the path. This voice sounds strangely similar at first:

> Let all who are simple come in here!
> Stolen water is sweet;
>> food eaten in secret is delicious! (Proverbs 9:16-17)

We look in her direction. A second beautiful woman vies for our attention. She, too, has a house on a hill. Her invitation sounds intriguingly tempting, promising secret delights.

We are pulled in two directions; which woman do we pursue? The book of Proverbs masterfully presents us with our dilemma. Do we pursue the first or the second woman? Who are these women? The text tells us the first is Wisdom and the second is Folly.

But who are Wisdom and Folly? The key comes from the location of their houses. They both have homes on hills. In the ancient Near East, including Israel, only one house could be built on a hill— God's house. It's clear from the context that Lady Wisdom is no other than God Himself. On the other hand, Folly stands for all the false gods, the idols, that compete for our attention.

We know that we must pursue the truth; that is our crucial starting place. The question is, do we pursue wisdom by pursuing God, or do we pursue wisdom by embracing idols of our own making?

A desire to follow. The New Testament continues to teach us about the source of true wisdom. Though no single book in the New Testament can be called a wisdom book (the book of James comes close), wisdom is an important topic to many of the New Testament writers because Jesus Christ's life epitomized wisdom.

Jesus manifested wisdom from the beginning of His life, and we are called to follow Him as its source. Luke's account of the Messiah's childhood notes more than once that "the child grew and became strong; He was filled with wisdom, and the grace of God was upon Him" (Luke 2:40,52). Mary and Joseph took Him to the temple when He was just a young child; He amazed the religious teachers with "His understanding and His answers" (Luke 2:47).

But Jesus was more than just a prodigal wise man. Paul made this clear when he wrote that Christ is the One "in whom are hidden all the treasures of wisdom and knowledge" (Colossians 2:3). Jesus is the beckoning figure of Wisdom in the beginning of Proverbs!

As Christians we're presented with a fundamental decision in daily living. Do we follow godly wisdom—allow ourselves to be led and discipled by Christ—or do we pursue the wisdom of this world in the form of modern idolatries?

To most people the latter course seems the most profitable and pursuing Christ the most unreasonable. But Paul opens our eyes to see that true wisdom flows not from secular philosophies but from the cross (1 Corinthians 1:18–2:16). To pursue true wisdom, to use Paul's words, is to "have the mind of Christ" (verse 16). In other words, we look at our circumstances from Christ's eternal perspective. We will then recognize that God is at work for our good in even the most tragic and difficult situations. As Oswald Chambers saw it, our dark moments may well be the shade of God's protecting hand:

Is my gloom, after all,
Shade of His hand,
outstretched caressingly?[2]

WISDOM'S POWER TO RE-ENVISION OUR LIVES

The wisdom literature of the Bible is a key ingredient in our spiritual growth. It is the means by which we develop a Christlike mind as we navigate life. The more we assimilate wisdom and avoid folly, which is the wisdom of the world, the more we will become like Christ — the goal of our spiritual development.

Does this mean that wise Christian men and women will live successful lives? Yes, but not necessarily in the areas most highly valued in our society. A wise Christian woman may be poor; a wise Christian man may be dying slowly and painfully of cancer. But their Wisdom, Christ, will be their solid rock of comfort and truth in the midst of tribulation's tossing waves.

Does this mean that wisdom does not lead to blessing, and folly does not lead to destruction? No, the Bible's teaching that the wise are blessed and the foolish destroyed is true when understood from the standpoint of eternity. *Perspective is the key.* Biblical wisdom allows us to "see through" to the larger picture. In other words, it broadens our vision of what is true about life and what is really the case when God looks at a thing.

We can understand this even in purely human terms. I recall this story from cancer specialist Dr. Bernie Siegel:

> This gentleman has a farm. He loves the old-fashioned way of doing things, so he doesn't have any mechanical equipment and plows his fields with a horse. One day as he was plowing his field, the horse dropped dead. Everyone in the village said, "Gee, what an awful thing to happen." He just responded, "We'll see." He was so at peace and so calm that we all got together and, because we admired his attitude so much, gave him a new horse as a gift. Then everyone's reaction was, "What a lucky man." And he said, "We'll see." A few days later the horse, being strange to his farm, jumped a fence and ran off, and everyone said, "Oh, poor fellow." He said, "We'll see." A week later the horse returned with a dozen wild horses following it. Everyone said, "What a lucky man." And he said, "We'll see." The next day his son went out riding, because now they had more than one horse, but the boy fell off the horse and broke his leg. Everyone said, "Oh, poor boy," but my friend said, "We'll see." The next day the army came to town taking all the young men for service, but they left his son

because of his broken leg. Everyone said, "What a lucky kid," and my friend said, "We'll see."[3]

None of us knows exactly how things are going to go from one moment to the next. Sometimes events that appear bleak suddenly transform themselves into the best news we could hope for. To live by true wisdom means that we can confidently take a "we'll see" attitude because we know that the whole of our life, from beginning to end, is in God's hands. He knows how events are unfolding, and He has already written the script with a complete and detailed ending. We can wait and see because we are convinced of His wisdom and good will toward us. All of His promises and plans will come to pass. That is how wisdom broadens our vision with heavenly perspective.

Psalm 73 is a wisdom psalm. The psalmist looked at his pitiful circumstances and compared them to the glowing success, wealth, and health of his ungodly neighbors and turned to God in anger and with envy. Then he paid a visit to the sanctuary and caught a glimpse of the glory of God. There he had a vision of the ultimate destiny of the wise and the foolish:

> Yet I am always with you;
> > You hold me by my right hand.
> You guide me with your counsel,
> > and afterward you will take me into glory.
> Whom have I in heaven but you?
> > And earth has nothing I desire besides you.
> My flesh and my heart may fail,
> > but God is the strength of my heart
> > and my portion forever.
>
> Those who are far from you will perish;
> > You destroy all who are unfaithful to you.
> But as for me, it is good to be near God.
> > I have made the Sovereign LORD my refuge;
> > I will tell of all your deeds. (Psalm 73:23-28)

The wise psalmist could praise God in the midst of his circumstances because he knew that God's intention toward him was loving and God's actions toward him were good.

READING WISDOM LITERATURE FOR SPIRITUAL GROWTH

We began this chapter with a glimpse of Job and his physical suffering as he stood at the brink of death. How does this story speak to you? When I was young, I had an intense fear of death. Though perfectly healthy, I knew that I could be struck with an incurable disease at any moment. I envisioned the world from my own perspective. I could only see the definite possibility of death and nothing beyond.

After I became a Christian, I looked at disease and death from God's perspective. I can't say that I don't worry about cancer or heart disease, but it no longer paralyses me because of my greater fear. The fear of the Lord makes me look at my life and the world from a higher perspective. What I see with my physical eyes is not all there is. Even if I do get a crippling or life-threatening disease, God will still be with me in my pain and suffering. And when I die, He will "take me into glory" (Psalm 73:24).

How is it with you? As you look around, have you noticed that you are living in a rather aimless generation? Our society has pushed God from the public square, and then we're surprised to find we have nothing to offer our young people in terms of standards of behavior or guidance for the future. Crime is on the rise and we desperately respond by executing more murderers and building more prisons. Why invest in moral education? How can we agree on whose values to teach? We come full circle: Where is wisdom to be found?

Such questions receive answers in the Scriptures, if we will read with open minds and hearts. How shall we read the wisdom literature for the greatest spiritual benefit? Here are a few suggestions to keep in mind:

- Read each passage in the light of its ever-expanding context—its immediate context, the context of the whole book, the context of all of the wisdom literature, and the context of the entire Bible. This principle, relevant for all biblical texts, is especially important to keep in mind for wisdom books, which often seem like a listing of disconnected sayings. It's also important to consider that individual proverbs, while generally true, are not directly applicable in every circumstance.
- Remember and apply the rules of poetry. Much wisdom, especially the proverbs, comes to us in poetic format. Proverbs often express common truths with striking metaphors that require significant reflection. Don't rush through them!

- Ask yourself, "What does *this* passage require of *me*?" A wisdom text will call you to think and act in new ways. Determine what the passage demands of your life, right now.
- Recognize that even the most practical bit of wisdom advice is a potent theological statement. Look at the first aphorism in the book of Proverbs, for example:

A wise son brings joy to his father,
but a foolish son grief to his mother. (Proverbs 10:1)

This proverb is typical in its contrast of wisdom and folly. Wisdom brings positive effects on the family, while foolishness brings negative effects. The proverb seems straightforward and clear. However, when read in context, we note strong theological overtones. Remember that this and the other proverbs follow Proverbs 1-9. In these chapters we have an association between wisdom and God on the one side, and folly and the idols on the other. Thus, children who bring joy to their parents demonstrate wisdom and show that they are on God's side, while those who bring grief show they have embraced folly, which means that, at heart, they are idolaters. What kind of child are you?

16

GOD'S COVENANT ENFORCERS

It was almost midnight when Julie opened the hotel door for her roommate, Lisa. She'd been a bit worried about her coworker, since they had an early morning flight the next day.

"Well, there you are! Why were you out so late tonight? Aren't you working on the 5:30 A.M. flight?"

"Yes, but today's horoscope told me that tonight I should 'be out and about.' It also said I should 'reach out to someone who's at a distance.' And here we are in Denver, so I thought I'd reach out to some old friends I haven't seen in a while."

"I wish you'd lay off that horoscope stuff. You take it way too seriously."

"Well, I'm just messing around with it. You don't think I'd make any serious decisions about my future based on the charts, do you? That would be crazy. No one can tell the future."

Mike and Kurt hadn't seen one another for a while, so they hung around after the Bible study to catch up. "Was that your son I saw in the paper making all-conference linebacker? That's awesome."

"Yeah, well I wish his grades were awesome, too. We're really worried about him getting into a decent school."

Mike moved closer and said in a quiet voice, "I'm not sure how much of a difference it's going to make anyway."

"What are you talking about?"

"I didn't want to bring this up in the Bible study, but I think that passage in Ezekiel is telling us the economy's going to crumble and our godless society is going to be thrown into chaos."

"Hey, I thought it was talking about ancient Babylonia."

Mike chuckled, "That's on the surface. I just got this great book, *Secret Prophecies Revealed.* It's a best-seller, and I tell you, my friend, it opens up the prophets."

Just as I was grabbing my briefcase to head for an appointment, someone knocked on my door. *Why can't they come during office hours?* I thought to myself.

When I opened the door, there stood a somber-faced Fred. He was usually outgoing, so a tinge of worry swept through my mind.

"Come on in, Fred. What's up? Did you want to talk about your paper?"

"Well, kind of. You see, I'm having trouble getting motivated."

"Why is that? You know you have to learn how to interpret the Bible correctly to preach, and I know you love to preach. I've heard you, and you're quite gifted." Fred was perhaps the most promising of all the seminary's present batch of students.

"That's just it. I'm not sure I'm called to the ministry, so I'm having trouble focusing on my seminary career."

"But Fred, you graduate this year and you already have your home church begging you to come back as an assistant."

"But Dr. Longman, I haven't heard the call. I mean, just last week you were lecturing on Isaiah and his clear-cut commission to proclaim God's Word to the people. I sure don't feel anything like that kind of guidance in my life."

I sighed inwardly. "Fred, I've got an appointment with the dean right now. How about lunch tomorrow? I'll even break my rule and pay for you. We have some talking to do."

Like any of us, Lisa, Mike, and Fred want to know what the future holds. All of us, to some degree, want to know what's going to happen so we can control it and avert pain and disaster.

Shall we go to the biblical prophets for this knowledge? That suggestion makes some Christians nervous. After all, God spoke so directly to His people in the past, but He doesn't seem to do that today. On the other hand, perhaps it would help to know a little more about the biblical prophets before making such broad generalizations.

Prophets show up throughout the Bible, from Abraham (see Genesis 20:7) to John (see Revelation 1:3). Some of them leave us an account in the biblical books that bear their names. Some of the prophets—like Samuel, Elijah, and Elisha—didn't write anything at all. (We'll see how important these so-called nonwriters were when we discuss the role of the prophet in the life of God's people.) And Moses, perhaps the most important prophet of all (see Deuteronomy 34:10), didn't write a prophecy, as such, but rather history and law.

Though prophecy stretched throughout the canonical period, the work of the prophets covers a narrow time period. Their work concentrated around the time of two major religious crises. First, in the eighth century B.C. God sent a number of prophets to warn His people of the coming disaster at the hands of the Assyrians (Joel,[1] Amos, Jonah, Hosea, Isaiah, Micah). Then, in the late seventh and early sixth centuries, He sent prophets once again to warn the people of the disaster involving the Babylonians (Jeremiah, Ezekiel, Zephaniah, Nahum, Habakkuk[2]). The last major flurry of prophecy took place during the time of uncertainty represented by the return to Judah after the Exile (Obadiah, Haggai, Zechariah, Malachi).

What's so important about these particular time periods? Why did God send the prophets then? *It is only as we understand the prophets' ancient role that we can apply their messages to our lives with integrity and power today.*

THE ROLE OF THE PROPHETS

The prophets are a richly diverse group. As one author expressed it:

> The Old Testament prophets were such a mixture of people that it is hard to find many similarities between them. Some were loners working independently, while others usually worked as part of a team. Some were skilled diplomats, at home at the highest levels of society, while others were blunt countrymen who didn't

seem to know the meaning of the word tact. Among them were quiet thinkers, eccentric dreamers, political activists, fierce accusers, and gentle encouragers.[3]

Their writings were also diverse. From Amos, we hear God's blunt, hard-hitting judgments—not only against the pagan nations that surround God's people, but toward Israel and Judah. Jeremiah, a reluctant and often angry prophet, speaks to God in plaintive tones. From Isaiah, we not only get threats and warnings but also some of the most beautiful and compelling pictures of God restoring His people to Himself. Nahum supernaturally anticipates the brutal destruction of Nineveh. Jonah tells the tragi-comedy of a prophet who believes he has a deeper sense of justice than the God who sends him on his mission.

What unites these characters and their varied messages? They are the servants of Yahweh and represent the One who guides the nations down through history. God sent the prophets to His people with urgent messages. The following biblical passage sets us on the right path to understanding who the prophets were.

The LORD warned Israel and Judah through all his prophets and seers: "Turn from your evil ways. Observe my commands and decrees, in accordance with the entire Law that I commanded your fathers to obey and that I delivered to you through my servants the prophets." (2 Kings 17:13)

THE PROPHETS ARE GOD'S MESSENGERS

There were no telephones, airmail services, fax machines, or e-mail messages in the ancient world. If an important memo had to go out, it was sent by surface mail—messengers walked, ran, and rode camels or horses. An ancient Near Eastern king had many messengers, and he would dispatch them through the world to tell the kings of lesser countries, and his subjects throughout his kingdom, how to behave. These messengers were the king's ambassadors, and they usually delivered their communications orally.

The prophets didn't get their assignment from human kings; they talked with the King of the Universe, who gave them messages to deliver to His servant people. So being a prophet was an awesome task. Scripture tells us that at his prophetic call, Isaiah was ushered into God's throne room where he saw the Lord and all His supernatural servants. Isaiah was overwhelmed and responded, "Woe to me! I am ruined! For I am a man of unclean lips, and I live among a people of unclean lips, and my eyes have seen the King, the LORD Almighty" (Isaiah 6:5). Then one of the angelic beings flew over to him with a burning coal and applied it to Isaiah's lips, symbolizing the fact that God was purifying him for his holy task. Isaiah was now ready, and he eagerly responded to the Lord's command to deliver His message of coming judgment and ultimate hope to Israel.

Not all the Lord's prophets were so agreeable. It was no easy task being the spokesman of the Lord. And prophets were out of work during the good times when everything was fine between God and His people. God sent the prophets when the people had turned their backs on Him. That's why the prophets were most active during the times mentioned above—periods of spiritual crisis when the message was: "Turn back from your evil ways, or die!" Thus, a more typical reaction than Isaiah's eagerness was the response of Moses during his commissioning at the burning bush: "O Lord, please send someone else to do it" (Exodus 4:13).

The prophet Jeremiah vividly expresses this internal struggle of the prophets. They were castigated by the people but could not keep from speaking because the Lord had given them the words to say. Jeremiah complained:

> O LORD, you deceived me, and I was deceived;
>   You overpowered me and prevailed.
> I am ridiculed all day long;
>   everyone mocks me.
> Whenever I speak, I cry out
>   proclaiming violence and destruction.
> So the word of the LORD has brought me
>   insult and reproach all day long.
> But if I say, "I will not mention him
>   or speak any more in his name,"
> His word is in my heart like a fire,
>   a fire shut up in my bones.
> I am weary of holding it in;
>   indeed, I cannot. (Jeremiah 20:7-9)

The most basic role of the prophets was to serve as God's messengers. They have been with the Lord in His heavenly throne room, and they've come back to the people to speak His words. We are to hear the prophets' words as if they were the very words of God. We are to obey the commands of the prophets as if they were God's commands. In fact, there's a close connection between God's Law and the message of the prophets. We could say, therefore, that the prophets are also God's lawyers.

THE PROPHETS AS LAWYERS

The legal profession doesn't enjoy a particularly good reputation in our society, but the lawyer metaphor does help us understand the actions of God's prophets. Specifically, the prophets entered the scene whenever Israel forgot, or ignored, their God and His laws.

Remember Elijah and Elisha? God sent them during the reign of Ahab, who had married Jezebel, the daughter of the priest-king of Baal. Being a zealous evangelist for her god in this new land, Jezebel was not content to worship Baal on her own. God sent Elijah and Elisha, two outstanding and powerful prophets, to counter the Baal threat and to warn both king and people of the dangers of following false gods. In a word, the prophets took up God's case against those who threatened His relationship with His people Israel. In the case of Elijah, it led to the famous showdown on Mount Carmel (1 Kings 18).

Do you remember that story? The contest was about whether God or Baal was more powerful, and the answer would be determined by discovering who could light the altar fire on top of the mountain. From a human perspective, the odds were stacked. There were 450 prophets of Baal to one prophet of God (1 Kings 18:22).

The prophets of Baal went first. If they succeeded, the contest would be over, and Elijah wouldn't even get his turn. Baal was the chief god of a polytheistic religious system. The Canaanites had hundreds of gods and each had its area of expertise. This contest focused on Baal's specialty—the weather. He was particularly adept at throwing down fire from heaven. A single lightning bolt would have done the trick in this challenge.

But, of course, the Baal prophets failed. After all, Baal was a figment of their imaginations. Those false prophets left the stage open for Elijah, who stepped forward and made things even more difficult by dousing the altar with water—not once, but three times! Elijah then offered a simple prayer, asking God to reveal His existence and power to the people who had turned their backs on Him. In immediate response, God sent fire from heaven and set the wet wood ablaze.

Elijah had come as a messenger-lawyer in a time of crisis, pressing

God's case against His people and the false gods to whom they had turned. In fact, sometimes the prophet's words came straight out of the ancient courtroom. Micah, another of God's prophetic lawyers, said:

> "Stand up, plead your case before the mountains;
>   let the hills hear what you have to say.
> Hear, O mountains, the LORD's accusation;
>   listen, you everlasting foundations of the earth.
> For the LORD has a case against his people;
>   He is lodging a charge against Israel." (Micah 6:1-2)

The prophets, as God's lawyers, brought a case against God's wandering people. Their goal was to get the people of God to leave their offensive idol worship and get back to their agreement with the one true God—to follow and worship Him.

THE PROPHETS AS THOSE WHO PRAY

The Bible tells us that the prophet's responsibility to pray for God's people was even more important than delivering God's message. First Samuel 12 is a major transitional point in the relationship between God and Israel. Up to this point Israel recognized God as the only king; their human ruler was a judge. But now God had made Saul their first king.

Samuel, who had served as judge, would no longer be the highest political authority in the land. He would take on an even more important role as a prophet—the one who would bring God's Word to His people. Samuel would serve as the conscience of the king when he began to think too much of himself and turn people toward himself rather than point them to the divine king.

At the moment of this transition, Samuel highlighted one task that was now his most important as God's prophet. At the end of the speech which inaugurated Saul as king and launched his prophetic career, Samuel said:

> Do not turn away after useless idols. They can do you no
> good, nor can they rescue you, because they are useless.
> For the sake of His great name the LORD will not reject His
> people, because the LORD was pleased to make you His
> own. As for me, far be it from me that I should sin against
> the LORD by failing to pray for you. And I will teach you the
> way that is good and right. (1 Samuel 12:21-23)

The prophets were master pray-ers. Abraham was the first person called a prophet in the context of praying for Abimelech's life. Pharaoh called on Moses the prophet to intercede with the Lord on behalf of Egypt (Exodus 8:8-15,25-32; 9:27-35; 10:16-20), and Moses pleaded for Israel after they sinned by worshiping the golden calf (32:30-34). Jeremiah prayed for the people (Jeremiah 18:18-20) until God forbade him to do so (7:16, 11:14, 14:11-12). Because the prophets were granted access to the very throne room of God, they had the responsibility to intercede on behalf of God's people.

THE PROPHET AS PREDICTOR

Now we come to the theme that opened this chapter. Yes, the biblical prophet is a messenger, a lawyer, a pray-er. But what about the prophet as predictor of the future? Isn't that what we commonly think of when we think of the prophets of the Bible? Don't the prophets present us with a vision of the future to tell us where history is heading?

I became a Christian during the fall of my first year of college. The more mature brothers and sisters (those who had been converted at least six months previously!) decided we should have a retreat.

It was a wonderful and memorable experience. In particular, I remember opening my Bible at random on a chilly evening as I sat by the fire. My eyes fell across the page to these words:

> Who has believed our message
> > and to whom has the arm of the LORD been revealed?
> He grew up before him like a tender shoot,
> > and like a root out of dry ground.
> He had no beauty or majesty to attract us to him,
> > nothing in his appearance that we should desire him.
> He was despised and rejected by men,
> > a man of sorrows, and familiar with suffering.
> Like one from whom men hide their faces
> > He was despised, and we esteemed him not.
> > > (Isaiah 53:1-3)

As I read on in this marvelous chapter, I realized that the prophet Isaiah was looking into the future and seeing Jesus, the person who had just come into my life as Savior and Lord. At that time I didn't know when these verses were written, but I knew this prophetic word came hundreds of years before Jesus actually lived. I can still remember the thrill of goose bumps as I thought about God's ability to see into the future. If God could control the future, then as one of His children, I could face it with certainty and confidence!

So, yes, the prophets saw into the future. God gave them glimpses of His plans for His people and His judgment for those who turned against Him. Isaiah made it clear that God's ability to see into the future and communicate it through His prophets was one of the things that differentiated the true God from all pretenders. Through His prophet, God challenged the idols.

> Who then is like me? Let him proclaim it.
>   Let him declare and lay out before me
> what has happened since I established my ancient people,
>   and what is yet to come—
>   yes, let him foretell what will come.
> Do not tremble, do not be afraid.
>   Did I not proclaim this and foretell it long ago?
> You are my witnesses. Is there any God besides me?
>   No, there is no other Rock; I know not one.
>   (Isaiah 44:7-8)

The prophets predicted the short-term future. Nahum, a prophet who prophesied sometime between 630 and 613 B.C vividly saw the destruction of Nineveh in 612 B.C.[4] The prophets looked into the far distant future as well, all the way to the end of history.

Yet our understanding of the prophets cannot end with the simple observation that they looked into the future. Too often we focus on the predictions of the prophets as the most important aspect of their work. We root out messianic prophecies to bolster our faith and to argue others into the kingdom of God. We look at the sometimes difficult prophetic imagery and try to figure out when the end of the world will come.

One of the best-selling books of all time claimed to unlock the prophecies of the end.[5] Such incredible interest and obsession puts the wrong color on our understanding of the ministry of the prophets. Douglas Stuart is surely not far off the mark when he claims that "less than 2 percent of Old Testament prophecy is messianic. Less than 5 percent specifically describes the New Covenant age. Less than 1 percent concerns events yet to come."[6]

In the biblical prophecies, the future is evoked in order to serve the purpose of the prophet's present. In other words, God revealed the future through the prophets in order to achieve an effect in the present. Sometimes God revealed the future in order to prevent coming disaster. For instance, God forced the reluctant prophet Jonah to go to Nineveh and tell the people there of coming disaster. They responded by changing their evil behavior and appealing to God for forgiveness.

Probably about a century later, God sent another prophet to speak a word about Nineveh. Nahum announced a judgment on the once-again wicked city, but this time its doom was certain. Why, in this case, did God reveal the future? Not to avert disaster, but to comfort His people who were living under the heel of that oppressive empire. In light of these considerations, it's clear that if we are to appreciate the biblical prophets we'll need to see them as more than just predictors of the future. They were also messengers, lawyers, and pray-ers.

But what possible benefit do their words have for us today? How do the prophets' messages affect life at the end of the twentieth century? Let's explore this further in the chapter ahead.

17

HEARING THEM TODAY

We read the Old Testament prophets with awe. They weren't like most people. God transported them to the very council chambers of heaven and revealed the future to them so they could guide the nations with boldness.

How do we read the prophets in the twentieth century? Do we pay attention only to the prophecies that predict the coming of the Messiah? And who, if anyone, is a prophetic voice today?

READING THE PROPHETS — RIGHT NOW

As we've learned, prophets were not out-of-touch visionaries with their eyes only on future realities. They saw the future for the sake of the present. The church has rightly canonized the particular prophetic writings in our Bible because their message carries beyond their own moment in time and is relevant for our faith and practice in the here and now.

Christians today are in the place of Israel in the past. Just as the prophets continually called Israel back into a faithful and obedient relationship with God, we're reminded, as we read God's Word through the prophets, of our responsibility to do the same. Like Israel, our tendency is to break covenant with God. We find substitutes—idols—that can take God's place. Our idols are different from those the ancient Israelites followed, but they're equally evil. The prophets remind us that to turn our backs on God and move toward false gods, such as money, power, sex, or pure self-interest, is to open ourselves to God's judgment.

Israel destroyed its national life by persisting in evil behavior. The people carelessly and continually broke God's law. We, too, show our rebellion against God by persisting in certain patterns of behavior that we know are displeasing to the Lord. Perhaps we can't seem to control our anger, so we leave ruined relationships in our wake. The prophets insist that we follow the Lord in all that we do to avoid ruining our lives.

If God's people ignore him, He will simply not allow them to live a satisfied, undisturbed life. But He will allow them to wander into unsafe pastures and taste the bitterness there. Perhaps the gnawing dissatisfaction that permeates a life apart from Him will cause them to come running back. And He will guide them into the one thing that quenches every yearning—fellowship with Himself. In this regard, I recall a probing question that writer C. S. Lewis once asked (and then answered): "Which of the religions of the world gives to its followers the greatest happiness? *While it lasts*, the religion of worshiping oneself is the best."[1]

But it doesn't last! As Lewis said elsewhere, "Our whole being by its very nature is one vast need; incomplete, preparatory, empty yet cluttered, crying out for Him who can untie things that are now knotted together and tie up things that are still dangling loose."[2] The prophets warned Israel to return to their first love for God, or they would experience God's absence in place of His blessing, spiritual knots and loose ends instead of peace. And they would continue to cry out in their deep neediness.

Perhaps they felt they were safe as long as the temple, the permanent residence of God, remained in their midst. Yet Jeremiah (chapter 7) warned the people that the temple was no guarantee of their safety. God was not bound by a building. Ezekiel (chapters 9-11) narrates God's abandonment of His temple.

Other prophets warned the people of Israel that their neglect of God would lead to their defeat and destruction. The book of Lamentations, for example, vividly pictures the horror that resulted because they refused to listen to the prophets.

The Old Testament prophets continue to serve as a reminder to us of our covenant relationship with God. They warn us that God must remain our top concern in life, more important to us than anything or anyone else. Our relationship with God is an exclusive one.

All too often, evil seems to come out on top—the bad guy wins. Those who ignore God seem to be the ones who have the money and the easy life. It was that way in the prophets' world, too. Their message reminds us who God is—holy and just—and that *present* reality is not *ultimate* reality. Both through their vision of coming judgment and their message of hope for those who follow God, the prophets tell us that God's people, who presently suffer, will ultimately enjoy living in His glorious presence.

Yes, God did reveal the future to the prophets. They saw historical events—battles, births, defeats, victories—years ahead of time. They saw the birth of a suffering Messiah (Isaiah 53) and even the end of the world (Isaiah 24–27). We read these prophecies and have an even greater sense of their truth since we can look back and see how many of the prophecies have come to pass. We marvel especially at the fulfillment of ancient prophecies at Christ's birth.

In their predictive capacity, the prophets show us that God is indeed in control of history. He is not bound by time as we are. When He reveals the future to us, it will come true; there's no doubt about it.

This is important to us because not all the prophecy of the Bible has been fulfilled. Yes, Jesus has died on the cross and has been raised. Yes, this spells defeat for Satan. But evil is still in the world. Through His old and His new prophetic word (the book of Revelation), God promises us that the end means total victory for God and His people and complete defeat for Satan. We can fully embrace this prophetic message of hope, and our confidence grows strong as we see God's track record displayed in the prophetic words of the past.

Yet as we think of the prophets as predictors, we may also be perplexed. If God spoke so marvelously through the prophets in the past, where are the prophets today?

IMITATING THE PROPHETS—ESPECIALLY JESUS

The prophet Joel (see verses 28-29) had a vision of hope for the future that went like this:

"And afterward,
  I will pour out my Spirit on all people.
Your sons and daughters will prophesy,
    your old men will dream dreams,
    your young men will see visions.
Even on my servants, both men and women,
    I will pour out my Spirit in those days."

Peter proclaimed these same words at Pentecost (Acts 2:17-21). God had just demonstrated His power to the crowds in Jerusalem through the Holy Spirit by empowering His people to speak in foreign languages. This event indicated that Joel's vision was being fulfilled in the events surrounding Jesus Christ.

Christians may disagree over the scope and precise interpretation of these verses, but my purpose is more narrow. Clearly, Peter is saying that God has now made prophets of all His people—male and female, young and old. All of us, therefore, must respond to the prophetic word by emulating the prophets. I'm not suggesting we wear loincloths and start eating locusts. And I don't think we should wear placards with the message, "The end is nigh!" But we, like the ancient prophets, are expected to hear the Word of God and speak it to others. We are commanded, according to Matthew 28:18-20, to make disciples, to baptize, and to teach what God has told us to teach. Like the prophets, we're commissioned to speak God's Word to others, and He has promised to be with us as we do.

Most of us will never experience God coming to us in a vision or hear Him speak audibly to us in the middle of the night. We have something much, much better—the Bible. The Bible is the Word of God that we prophetically proclaim to the world. The book of Hebrews tells us we have something superior to the prophets—we live in the day in which God speaks through His very own Son (1:1-4)!

Thanks to the Bible we can look into the future and say without a shadow of a doubt, "The end is coming! Be ready! Jesus is coming soon." And we must call people to turn away from their evil ways and embrace the one true God. We are God's prophets as we proclaim His Word to a fallen, evil world.

We are prophets in another sense as we pray for God's people. Abraham, Moses, Samuel, Jeremiah, and the other prophets prayed for God's mercy and compassion on their world, and we can do the same. When we pray for our future and for the future of the church, we engage in a powerful, prophetic ministry that few Christians take full advantage of.

In the book of Deuteronomy, God tells His people how to distinguish true prophecy from false (chapter 13, 18:14-22). He says that He will raise up a line of prophets to follow Moses who will bring them His word. He states this promise in such a way that the people soon expected one great prophet who would be the climax to this line: "I will raise up for them a prophet like you from among their brothers; I will put My words in his mouth, and he will tell them everything I command him. If anyone does not listen to My words that the prophet speaks in My name, I Myself will call him to account" (Deuteronomy 18:19-20). Thus, in a sermon recorded in the book of Acts (2:14-36), Peter bears witness that not only is Jesus the ultimate object of prophecy, He is also the greatest prophet of all.

As we seek to imitate the prophets, we imitate Jesus.

PROFITABLE READING — IN THE PROPHETS!

All too often, modern readers are put off by the length and complexity of the prophetic writings. Has that ever happened to you? I recall times in my own life when reading prophetic writings struck me as particularly strange and difficult. It's true that really to hear the prophets in their original setting we need to do some hard listening, but the message is worth it. If you want to hear and appropriate the message of God's servants to full benefit, perhaps the following study principles can serve as a guide:

- Read the passage in context. This reminder, so important for all Bible reading, is particularly significant when we read the prophets. The structure of prophetic books may well elude us upon a surface reading. In a pronouncement commonly attributed to Martin Luther, we hear this about the prophets: "They have a queer way of talking, like people who, instead of proceeding in an orderly manner, ramble off from one thing to the next, so that you cannot make head nor tail of them or see what they are getting at."

Does that mesh with your experience of the prophets? Most prophetic books are a collection of sermons from throughout the prophet's career. They are often arranged topically, not chronologically. So we may get the initial impression of a hodgepodge of oracles. This leads to our second guideline.

- Get a sense of the overall outline. If you feel lost and can't figure out how a passage fits into the overall context or where the prophet is going with his message, have an outline of the whole book in front of you. Any reader can do this by closely analyzing transitions and relationships between sections but don't hesitate to use a good commentary for this purpose as well.
- Know the historical setting. The prophets looked into the future to serve the purposes of the present. To understand prophecy, it's important to have an idea of when the prophet lived and to know what was going on at the time they were speaking.

The prophets, more than any other writers of the Bible, usually tell us when they lived and preached. Look at the first verse, the superscription, which typically gives the names of the kings who lived during the prophet's "term of office." By then turning to the historical books, you can get a better understanding of context in the events surrounding the prophecy. A good commentary or even a Bible history book will summarize this material. The point is that the prophets do not free-float through history; their message is firmly grounded in contemporary events.

- Review and utilize the guidelines for interpreting poetry. God wanted to capture peoples' imaginations as well as their intellects, so the prophets often used poetry's parallelism and striking images to deliver the message.

With these guidelines in mind, we now can ask a series of questions of any particular text in order to get to the heart of its meaning:

Is the prophet speaking of the present or the future? Don't assume the prophet is predicting the future in the passage you are studying. It's much more likely that he's addressing the immediate situation of his audience.

Is the prophecy literal or figurative? Sometimes we have to be open to either a literal or figurative fulfillment of prophecy. We can't just assume one or the other.[3] The problem with most religious people at the time of Christ's first coming was that they had the prophecy all figured out; they thought they knew exactly how it would be fulfilled. So when Jesus came, they didn't recognize Him. As we look at how Old Testament prophecy was fulfilled in the first coming of Christ, we see instances of literal and figurative fulfillment.

Is the prophetic prediction conditional or unconditional? When the prophet looked to the future, he sometimes saw what God would certainly do. God would not change His mind; the prophetic message was a pronouncement of judgment and salvation (Nahum, Daniel 7–12). At other times, the prophet painted a picture of the future that served as a warning to the people. If they obeyed God, they could avoid the announced judgment (Jonah).

What is the possibility of multiple fulfillment? Prophets who spoke the Word of God always saw the future accurately. But they didn't fully understand what God had given them to say. The fulfillment of their prophetic word often happened in stages, leading up to the final fulfillment. In other words, the Old Testament prophets spoke frequently of a coming "Day of the Lord." This was a day when God's enemies would be judged and His people would be saved. As we read all the passages in the Bible today, we know that the prophets had one ultimate day in mind, the day of final judgment—the day when Christ would return at the end of history (Joel 2:28-32, Amos 5:18-20, Zephaniah).

But this final, consummate Day was played out in particular "days"—or periods of time throughout history, according to the Bible. Such days were either *called* the Day of the Lord or *described* as if they were that Day. For instance, when the Babylonians destroyed Jerusalem, it was the Day of the Lord (Lamentations 1:12,21; 2:16). When Jesus died, events associated with the Day took place (Matthew 27:45-56). In the New Testament, it is the day Christ returns again which is *the* Day, the ultimate fulfillment.

Have I remembered the primary goal of prophecy? This is the final and most important question we can ask as we interpret prophecy. Prophecy was not given to provide the material for speculation about the future or to reveal secret information from which we can predict the end of history. Prophecy centers on Jesus Christ, the Messiah. Paul said that all promises find their "Amen" in the Son of God (2 Corinthians 1:20). As you read the prophets, look for His incomparable goodness and grace to shine through in everything they say.

18

MANUALS FOR DISCIPLESHIP

"I want to be like Jesus, but I'm more like Peter."

That caught Rebecca's attention. Up to that point, her conversation with Linda had been pretty ho-hum. "What do you mean?"

"Well, you know, as Christians, we're supposed to act like Christ. But I seem to act more like one of the dull-witted disciples."

"Give me an example, Rebecca."

"Well, yesterday I get this great opportunity to share the gospel with my boss, and I get all nervous and don't say a word. What kind of disciple am I anyway?"

"I don't know," Rebecca said. "I feel exactly the same way. I wish there was a manual somewhere on what it meant to follow Jesus. You don't know any good books about it, do you?"

TRY THE GOSPELS!

Rebecca and Linda are like most of us. We want to follow Christ, but we struggle and need help. There are many good books on what it means to be a disciple of Christ, but the biblical Gospels are our primary manuals of discipleship. The New Testament opens with these four books that share remarkable similarities—as well as striking differences. Since they tell the story of the life and death of Jesus the Messiah, they are in many ways the heart of the Christian faith and the most often read portion of the Bible.

The Gospels are realistic books. They don't present the Christian life as always successful and vibrant. Peter and the other disciples had their wonderful moments of faith and boldness as well as their failures. At times they turned their backs on the Lord and their faith. Because of this, the disciples inspire us to new levels of spiritual growth and also encourage us to deeper discipleship when we learn how they struggled, failed, and then got back on their feet.

But what, exactly, is a gospel? The word itself is a translation of a Greek term that means "good news." Thus, the Gospels present the good news that God has sent His Son, Jesus, to die on the cross in our place. And the form of the presentation is actually a literary genre with certain distinctive characteristics. Most scholars today believe that the Gospels follow a pattern similar to ancient Greco-Roman biographies.[1] They don't cover Jesus' whole life; they concentrate only on the last three years, especially highlighting His death and resurrection. But these writings still have the feel of an ancient biography rather than a modern one.

Why do the Gospels repeat each other in telling the story of Jesus? This question comes to the fore as we consider how similar these four books are.[2] As we compare them, we often hear the same episode two, three, and occasionally, even four times.[3] But it's also true that we learn new things about Jesus in each of the Gospels. For instance, we only hear about Jesus' birth in Matthew (1:18-25) and Luke (2:1-7). Only in Matthew do we learn of the wise men (2:1-12). So these books are not carbon copies of each other after all. Even when they tell the same story, they do it with a different twist. We might think of them as four different "takes" on the same scene.

> Imagine four famous painters. Let's imagine we're talking about each of these artists as having painted essentially the same scene. First, there's Monet with the Impressionist's version, as if he had used small bird feathers for paint. At

least, that's how it looks to a novice from a distance. Van Gogh's version of the same scene might look to a child as if he had painted on the canvas many long worms lying side by side.

Leonardo da Vinci might make the conservative art viewer feel that he is back in the realm of reality—with more lifelike dimensions. In other words, the painting is looking increasingly like a photograph. Then, for a fourth view, we might select a more bizarre modernist version of the same scene.

Four literary painters interpreting the same subject—that's what we find in our Gospels. Consequently, while we see great areas of overlap in the Gospels, we are also able to distinguish the earmarks of the individual writers in their art of historical treatment.[4]

Each gospel story has a divinely inspired slant on the life of Jesus and its meaning for us as disciples. And because each tells the story to a different original audience, we learn something new in each one. But the Gospels do more than tell us about Jesus' life; they are manuals of discipleship. They give us a clear picture of Jesus' actions and teachings so that we may follow in His steps.

Before we get into the contents of the Gospels, let's get an overview of the four individual stories we know as the gospels of Matthew, Mark, Luke (with Acts), and John. For if we want to grow as disciples of Christ, we must become students of these portraits of Jesus. They were written for people like you and me who want our lives to reflect Christ's glory.

Second-century theologian Irenaeus, in *Against Heresies*, captured the flavor of the unity and diversity of the Gospels by likening each to one of the faces of the cherubim described in Ezekiel 1:10: Matthew, the ox; Mark, the lion; Luke, the man; and John, the eagle. Using his designations, we can see how each gospel's distinctive angle focuses on a particular aspect of being a disciple of Jesus.

MATTHEW: THE OX

While most people think that Mark was the first gospel written,[5] the book of Matthew appears first in our New Testament. Appropriately, the first chapter of Matthew opens with a genealogy. Unlike the genealogies in the other gospels, Matthew's begins with Abraham, the father of the Israelite nation, and ends with Jesus Christ. This highlights an important theme of Matthew's gospel: *Jesus is the fulfillment of all the promises of the Old Testament.*

Irenaeus appropriately likens the book to the ox, since the gospel "tells us of His work as our High Priest—and reminds us that He himself is our sacrifice!"[6] This gospel bridges the gap between the Old and the New Testaments. Yes, Matthew proclaims, something new and exciting is happening in Jesus, but it is the fulfillment, not the rejection, of the past (Matthew 5:17-20).

Matthew, like all biblical books, was not written abstractly for all believers. It was written specifically for a particular group of people. From its message, we can be fairly certain that Matthew is speaking to a Jewish audience. He wants them to recognize that Jesus is the fulfillment of all their long-awaited expectations. Not only does his genealogy support this concern; Matthew constantly quotes the Old Testament, applying it to the life of Jesus to show that Jesus is the object of the age-old prophecies found there. He cites these prophecies and pronounces them "fulfilled" in Jesus (for instance, see 2:17-18, 3:1-3, 4:14-16).

Matthew, in 2:5-6, declares outright to his readers that Jesus is the Messiah (that is, "the anointed one," the Hebrew equivalent of the Greek term for "Christ") in fulfillment of Micah 5:2. Jesus is the expected Jewish Messiah, the One who was coming to save Israel from their oppression and trouble.

Matthew even has a distinctive Jewish-oriented structure to his gospel. He has arranged the story of Jesus into five parts, each part composed of a description of what Jesus did, followed by a report of His teaching. The fivefold structure of Matthew's gospel may intend to reflect the fivefold Torah, the first five books of the Bible, implicitly claiming that Christians have a new Torah or foundation to their religion. The "story" of Jesus unfolds in chapters 1–4, 8–9, 11–12, 13:54–17:27, 19–22. The "teachings" come in chapters 5–7, 10, 13:1-53, 18, and 23–28.

Matthew also has a distinctive slant on what it means to follow Jesus. For Matthew, discipleship requires radical obedience to Jesus' teachings. The Sermon on the Mount (5–7) is an ethical primer for Jesus' followers, showing how their faith should shape their lives. In these chapters and throughout the book, Matthew provides us with a clear guide to our behavior as disciples of Jesus. However, Matthew also recognizes that disciples are not Jesus Himself; that is, disciples are not perfect as He is.

Peter incarnates the life of the imperfect disciple. As Genesis follows the story of Abraham, the Gospels follow the story of Peter because he is an integral part of Jesus' ministry and a mirror image of our lives as disciples. Like Peter, we fail as well as succeed in following Christ. One moment Peter trusts Jesus with his whole heart, the next he doubts Him and needs a rebuke. Peter's impulsive spirit comes through most vividly when Jesus walks on the water (Matthew 14:22-36). In response to his Lord's invitation, Peter boldly steps out of the boat and starts walking toward Jesus on the water's surface. But he's distracted by the chaos of the waves and takes his focus off the One empowering him. At that moment he begins to sink.

Can you relate to that kind of lapse in faith? Like Peter, at one moment we trust and follow wholeheartedly; at another, when the pressure builds, we sink into doubt and despair. Peter's story can encourage us, though, because we see that his lapses in no way destroyed his relationship with Jesus. They simply became teaching tools in the hands of the Master Teacher.

Finally, it is Matthew who gives us the clearest of all the discipleship mandates—the verse we call the Great Commission. Matthew 28:18-20 not only calls us to be disciples; it requires us to make disciples of others as well.

MARK: THE LION

According to Irenaeus, Mark is the lion-gospel because it "tells us of the princely work of Christ, who comes to rule the nations." In terms of chronology, Mark was probably the first gospel written and was used by Matthew and Luke as they wrote their accounts of the life, death, and resurrection of Jesus Christ. Just as Matthew was originally written for an audience with a Jewish background, Mark was written for a Christian audience.

Mark is the shortest of the Gospels. It's also, in many ways, the most exciting. Mark tells the story in short, quick episodes. The Greek term for *immediately* appears often in the original text. Something important is happening—and it's happening quickly!

The opening clearly states that the book is "the gospel about Jesus Christ, the Son of God" (Mark 1:1). It also asserts, by quoting Isaiah, that this is the long-awaited gospel story. In this way, Mark shows that, while something new and exciting is on the scene, it is the continuation of the story begun in the Old Testament.

As Mark narrates, we immediately see that many people failed to recognize Jesus' special status. During His lifetime His messiahship came enveloped in secrecy. Jesus would exorcise the possessed but then command the demons not to tell anyone who He was (1:25,34). He healed the sick but then demanded that they keep silent about it (1:44). From this gospel we sense that something marvelous—but not yet fully revealed—was underway.

The disciples were slow to understand. They were not brilliant followers of the Lord. They had materialistic expectations, but Jesus told them the true road of the disciple is not a highway leading straight to worldly glory; rather, it is a pathway of suffering (9:33-37). After all, their master, whom they were following, achieved glory only after a life of rejection climaxed by an excruciating death. So this is the message of Mark for Jesus' disciples in the countless generations after His death and resurrection: *Glory comes only on the path of suffering and only through the life of a servant.*

LUKE: THE MAN

Luke, the third account of the Gospels, is the only gospel with a sequel. We often lose sight of the fact that the book of Acts is really "Luke: Part 2," since the gospel of John stands between the two. However, the first verse of Acts makes it obvious that it is a continuation of the story begun in Luke.

The focus of Luke–Acts is God's plan to bring salvation to all of God's people. Perhaps this is why Irenaeus called it the gospel with the face of a man, which speaks of how Jesus "took on our humanity in His compassion for us in our fallen state." The story follows the work of the Holy Spirit from the time Jesus is born until the start of the church and its spreading influence (not just in Palestine but throughout the Gentile world).

Even without Acts, Luke is the longest gospel of all. More than half of its contents are unique to the other three gospels. Yet Luke's gospel reads like a personal conversation with a person named Theophilus.[7] What will they talk about? Luke intended to offer an orderly and accurate account of the life of Jesus and the rise of the early church in order that Theophilus might "know the certainty of the things you have been taught" (1:4). He said that he based his account on a careful investigation and assessment of the reports of eyewitnesses.

His intentions are historical, but also theological and ethical. New Testament scholar Daryl Bock analyzes the special intention of the gospel of Luke by reading the introduction carefully (1:1-4) and analyzing the nature of its content. [8] He views Theophilus as a real person, an individual who represents Gentiles who are wondering where they fit into God's plan of salvation. Since the time of Abraham, Gentiles have been outsiders; now God is reaching out to them in a new and exciting way. But questions would arise in the minds of Jewish Christians as well as Gentile Christians, and Luke seeks to answer these questions by looking at the life of Christ.

What is the basic structure of the book? Literary scholar Michael Travers suggests that the gospel of Luke is an "archetypal quest story."[9] That is, it follows the exploits of its hero, namely Jesus, as He goes from adventure to adventure in order to accomplish the object of His "quest," the salvation of His people. Far from trivializing Jesus' life, reading this gospel as an adventure story uncovers the excitement of it. Jesus encounters threatening obstacles to the fulfillment of His task, most blatantly in His conflict with the demonic world. But He defeats their threat to reach the cross and accomplishes God's salvation. The book of Acts shows how Jesus' accomplishment was for the salvation of Gentiles as well, and that it led to the formation of His church—not just for Jewish people but for all people of the world.

Acts, too, is like a quest. This time it's the Holy Spirit's quest, triumphing over various obstacles, such as age-old prejudices against Gentiles. Jesus and the Holy Spirit work through the disciples-apostles to reach their goal.

Michael Wilkins, in his study of discipleship, shows that Luke's special contribution is to depict the life of Jesus—and the life of the Christian disciple—as being a journey.[10] In Acts, Christianity is called the Way (9:2), and a disciple is someone who follows in the Way of Jesus. Perhaps this language comes from the Wisdom literature of the Old Testament, where following the way of God, the way of Wisdom, is likened to being on the right path. Luke's call to discipleship, then, is *to get on the road of life by faith in Jesus Christ, the One who leads the way.* This way of following, by Jesus' example and teaching, leads to a life that denies the self.

JOHN: THE EAGLE

Whenever I read the first few verses of the gospel of John I get the impression that John stands at a distance from the first three gospels. He still tells the story of Jesus' life and ministry, but his distinctive emphases and concerns stand out when studied on the background of the three synoptic Gospels.

For one thing, the gospel of John looks at Jesus' life with the full knowledge that He was the very Son of God, in the special way that later Christian theology described as being the second person of the

Trinity. Irenaeus associates this gospel with the eagle, "telling us that Spirit is flown forth from the Father and broods protectively over His people, the Church."

In a bold move, John opens his gospel with these well-known words: "In the beginning was the Word, and the Word was with God, and the Word was God" (1:1). The Word is soon to be identified as Jesus in verse 14: "the Word became flesh and made his dwelling among us." Jesus reveals the glory of God to us because He is God Himself.

At the end of the book, the author of John makes his intention crystal-clear to his readers. He wrote so that the reader "may believe that Jesus is the Christ, the Son of God, and that by believing you may have life in His name" (20:31). Jesus is life and He brings life to His disciples—and to the whole dying world.

The disciple in John's gospel is someone who *turns to Jesus to find life.* According to Simon Peter, only Jesus has "the words of eternal life" (6:68). Disciples are those who cling to Jesus as a branch does to a vine, and then they show the life-giving connection by living a productive and meaningful life (15:5-11). Further, *the disciple lives by love, not just love for God, but love for others* (13:34-35).

FOLLOWING JESUS

In light of these four "takes" on what it means to follow Jesus, what kind of disciple are you? If you have a moment right now, think through your approach to following Jesus: Which of the gospels most powerfully resonates with your own personality? Any of us might benefit by asking ourselves another simple question in this regard: If I were asked to paint a portrait of Jesus, what would my view of Him emphasize? Think about the following:

- What stands out to me as most attractive in His life and character?
- What do I see in Him that I wish to emulate in my own life?
- What is it about Him that inspires me to sacrifice my life on His behalf?

Clearly, following Jesus is a radical calling, just as Matthew said it ought to be. It will demand everything from us as we travel down the path of life with Him. Yet He leads us one step at a time and gives us the strength to keep going, even when our motives are less than pure.

So don't be discouraged by the inevitable faltering steps or the stops-and-starts that may characterize your own commitment today. "I am with you always, to the very end of the age," Jesus said. He is there to lift us up and set us on the road again and again. I like the way writer Frederick Buechner put it in his book *The Magnificent Defeat*:

> The voice that we hear over our shoulders never says, "First be sure that your motives are pure and selfless and then follow me." If it did, then we could none of us follow. So when later the voice says, "Take up your cross and follow me," at least part of what is meant by "cross" is our realization that we are seldom any less than nine parts fake. Yet our feet can insist on answering Him anyway. And on we go, step after step.[11]

19

FOLLOWING OUR WARRIOR-TEACHER

G od as warrior?

Yes! He led His people through the Red Sea and then crushed the Egyptian army with a cataclysmic ambush. He smashed down the imposing walls of Jericho and condemned the city to a fiery end. Over and over the people of God were oppressed by one pagan nation after another: the Babylonians, the Persians, the Greeks, and finally the Romans. And their God warred against all of them.

But Jesus as warrior?

Yes again!

JESUS ASSAULTS THE EVIL KINGDOM
At the end of the Old Testament period, the prophets saw that Israel's history was going to be the story of one oppression after another, but they also saw a flash of

hope at the end. Daniel (Chapter 7) and Zechariah (Chapter 14), among others, looked into the future and saw that God would once again come as a warrior and bring an end to His people's suffering. This is the note on which the Old Testament ends: *The divine warrior is coming again.*

The Gospels richly present Jesus and His life. It would be impossible to describe here everything about Him and His significance to us. For that reason, I've chosen to look at two perspectives that run through all the Gospels—Jesus the Warrior and Jesus the Teacher.

When the New Testament opens with the four Gospels, a new phase of God's plan of salvation begins. It's been about four hundred years since the last prophets spoke, but the first words we hear from the New Testament sound eerily similar to those of the ancient preachers. John the Baptist looks at the people coming to him for baptism and says,

> "The ax is already at the root of the trees, and every tree
> that does not produce good fruit will be cut down and
> thrown into the fire. . . . But after me will come one who is
> more powerful than I. . . . His winnowing fork is in his
> hand, and he will clear his threshing floor, gathering his
> wheat into the barn and burning up the chaff with
> unquenchable fire." (Matthew 3:10-12)

John expected God to destroy the enemies of the faith and to save God's faithful followers. He expected the divine warrior.

According to the Gospels, Jesus then came to John at the Jordan River. John recognizes Jesus as the one he is expecting and baptizes Him. At this point John leaves the public eye and Jesus' ministry takes center stage.

John, thrown into prison by Herod, receives what are to him disturbing reports. Jesus isn't leading a revolt against the Romans. He's not uprooting hypocritical Jewish leaders. Instead, He's healing the sick, exorcising demons, and preaching the good news to the poor! John now doubts his choice. He wonders whether Jesus is the right one. So he sends two of his disciples to Jesus with the burning question, "Are you the one who was to come, or should we expect someone else?" (Matthew 11:3).

Jesus responds, but He doesn't answer with words. He speaks by taking John's disciples with Him and doing more of the same: He heals; He raises the dead; and He preaches the good news to the poor.

By these actions He communicates to John, "Yes, I am the one you were expecting. I am the divine warrior. But, John, I've come to fight more than flesh-and-blood enemies; I've come to fight Satan himself."

Jesus' actions in the Gospels are an assault on Satan's kingdom. We can see this in the numerous stories of exorcism. Jesus always wins the skirmish — the demons are afraid of Him because they know He's more powerful. Jesus further advances the war as He preaches the good news and people are taken out of Satan's grasp to become part of God's kingdom.

All of Jesus' ministry is simply a prelude to the cross. If we're alert as we read, we'll see that the real focus of the four Gospels is the passion story — the events leading up to and climaxing in Jesus' death. Jesus thus wins the war, not by killing someone else but by dying Himself. The Cross is the ultimate victory over Satan.

WE CONTINUE THE FIGHT

Peter tried to win the spiritual battle with a sword (Matthew 26:47-56). Jesus tells him to put away his weapon; the battle will be won on the cross. And indeed, as Paul describes it, Jesus did win the battle on the cross where He "triumphed" over the "powers and authorities" (Colossians 2:15).

While Jesus' victory means that the ultimate outcome of the war is certain, the battle still isn't over. As Ephesians describes it, our own lives are in a battle against the spiritual powers and principalities (Ephesians 6:10-20). The Gospels invite us to "put on the armor of God" and follow Jesus by fighting in His army.

Unlike soldiers in human warfare, Christians are soldiers who know, thanks to the Cross, that the ultimate outcome of the war is in their favor. We look forward with certainty to the day of complete victory at the end of time (See Revelation 19:11-16). Until then we struggle confidently in the present evil world.

Just as Jesus told Peter to put away his sword (John 18:10-11), we learn that our weapons are not physical; they are spiritual. According to Paul in Ephesians 6:10-20, our powerful weapons are faith, hope, love, and the Word of God. The true disciple who follows Jesus' actions as displayed in the Gospels is a soldier in the army of God. We pray, preach, and love so that the kingdom of Satan might topple.

Where do we follow Jesus into the battle today? There are three battle fronts facing the contemporary Christian warrior. First, *the world* is an evil and dangerous place. Injustices abound; diseases rage; wars decimate. Spiritual warfare doesn't mean exorcising demons. It means getting into the real world and battling the forces that stand against God. God has given each of us a part in the battle. We are all in the midst of the chaos, and we need to look for opportunities to turn back the forces of evil. And we must keep two principles in mind as we engage in this battle. One is that we fight not in our own power but in the power of Christ. This means we can have confidence as we enter the fray against forces that are clearly more powerful than we are. We must also remember that our weapons are spiritual. Prayer is much more powerful than a gun; love is more persuasive than violence.

The second battle front is *the hearts of others*. This is our struggle to evangelize those who need Christ. The world is clearly divided into two realms—those who stand with Jesus and those who stand against Him by standing with Satan. The most severe damage we can bring to Satan's kingdom is to share the gospel of peace with those who are in his army. When they hear it and believe it, they change armies! They defect from Satan's army and join the army of Christ.

Third, the fiercest battleground is *our own hearts*. All honest Christians know they still struggle with sin in their attitudes and actions. While we seek to remove the speck from our brother's eye, we need to see the log in our own (Matthew 7:4-5). While the Christian life is a great victory, it is also a war against the evil that remains in us. But our hopes are lifted as we remember that it is Jesus who gives us the weapons to fight the battle.[1]

JESUS TEACHES ABOUT ANOTHER KINGDOM

Jesus the Warrior-Savior and Jesus the Teacher are one and the same. The Jesus who died on the cross and defeated Satan is the same Jesus who preached to the multitudes and taught His disciples. Some people have trouble with a Jesus who claims to be God and went to the cross, but they love the Jesus who taught such high ethical standards and pronounced such lofty humanitarian principles. Of course, these are the same folks who may conveniently forget Jesus' teachings on social and individual justice. They cling to Jesus the Savior and forget that He also taught us to act in a certain way. We need to see that there is only one Jesus Christ, and if we are to follow Him, we must know what He did *and* what He taught.

Jesus' teaching is so wide-ranging, rich, and powerful that it's impossible to do more than hint at it in this chapter. And we must study all four gospels to hear Jesus' teaching. The Gospels sometimes repeat His teaching verbatim, but at other times they complement and enrich each other. Nevertheless, we ought to look at Jesus' sayings within the context of the gospel in which they appear. The differences often support the distinctive theological contribution of the individual gospel. It's wrong to try to immediately harmonize the various gospel reports or to try to get behind them to "what Jesus really said."

Let's cut right to the heart of *how* Jesus taught and *what* He taught. First we'll look at the parable, Jesus' most distinctive teaching style, and then we'll look at the heart of His message—the kingdom of God.

The parable—a distinctive style. Certainly Jesus used other forms of speech, as shown by the Sermon on the Mount (Matthew 5-7), but He often used parables to communicate His message. Jesus did not invent the parable form, so why did He use it?

He never tells us directly, though He does hint at His motivations for speaking this way. The parable form comes through in the Old Testament (see Judges 9:7-15, 2 Samuel 12:1-10) and was part of the teaching repertoire of the Jewish sages. So, by using the parable form, Jesus claims to be a teacher in the wisdom tradition of the Old Testament. We are to sit at His feet and listen to His authoritative teaching.

The parable suited Jesus' purpose for other reasons. It offered glimpses of realities that people were not prepared to understand in their entirety. Parables both revealed truths about the kingdom of God and at the same time shrouded it in mystery. The parable was the ideal teaching vehicle for subjects beyond human comprehension. Parables speak to us in a poetic language of picture images. The parables teach us about things we don't know by comparing them to things we do know in our everyday experience.

For example, Jesus began one well-known parable with, "The kingdom of heaven is like a mustard seed." His hearers had all seen a mustard seed, while perhaps knowing little about the kingdom of God. But as Jesus led them through the comparison "Though it is the smallest of all your seeds, yet when it grows, it is the largest of garden plants and becomes a tree" (Matthew 13:31-32), they learned more about the kingdom. That is, though small at the time He was speaking, the kingdom of God would expand until it encompassed all the world.

To say that the kingdom of God is like a mustard seed takes hold of our imaginations much more readily than the nearly equivalent statement, "The kingdom is small now, but it's going to grow." The parable's story-like format compels our interest and gets us to think about God and the reality of the spiritual world.

Not all characters, events, and objects of a parable have symbolic value. They are not secret codes to be unlocked. They may have more than one point, but their interpretation arises naturally out of the comparison made (the nature of the mustard seed with the kingdom of God, for example). So the parable form reveals, yet also shrouds, the ultimate truths of the kingdom of God, a frequent topic of Jesus' parables.

God's kingdom — the heart of the message. Jesus proclaims that He has brought the kingdom of God to earth but that it will also come in the future. He further instructs people how they should act as His disciples in light of this truth.

In Matthew 12:29 Jesus utters a brief parable teaching that the kingdom of God is present. He reveals that His ability to cast out demons is based on His overcoming Satan himself. In the previous verse He states it more directly: "If I drive out demons by the Spirit of God, then the kingdom of God has come upon you."

Jesus then informs us that by following Him we align ourselves with the kingdom of God rather than with Satan's kingdom. The kingdom of God, after all, is God's rule over all things. So the parables teach that God's kingdom is here in seed form, but not yet here in its full-blown form. In time it will grow to universal proportions. We live in the kingdom of God, but we also await its full manifestation.

The parables that emphasize the presence of the kingdom encourage us by revealing that God is present with us in our daily struggles. The parables that emphasize the future completion of the kingdom alert us to be prepared, to live wisely, and act in a way that pleases God in the present.

Jesus' teaching, particularly His use of parables, with its focus on the kingdom of God and living as disciples of Christ, are infinitely rich and deserve a lifetime of contemplation.

READING THE GOSPELS FOR SPIRITUAL GROWTH

The Gospels are similar to Old Testament historical narrative, so when you read the Gospels, you can use the same principles of reading narrative suggested at the end of chapter 9, "History: Learning the Lessons of the Past." Also, follow these guidelines:

- Remember that the Gospels' biographies are not exactly like modern biographies. Don't press the Gospels for chronological details or expect that you will learn Jesus' exact words.

- Read each gospel separately before reading them together. The four Gospels convey complementary perspectives on Jesus' words and deeds. Don't force them into a single mold.

- When reading the parables, research the object of comparison in its original historical setting to help illuminate its message. Parables are not secret codes, nor do they have only one single meaning. The parable itself often gives guidance as to its meaning.

- Be on the lookout for connections to the Old Testament. The Gospels are not a new beginning; they are the fulfillment of predictions, themes, and types from the Old Testament.

- Finally, remember that the Gospels are not simply historical reports. They were written after Jesus' death in such a way that they apply His actions and deeds to the life of the church. The Gospels do, indeed, tell of history, but they also preach to us. The descriptions of the disciples' actions teach us about the ups and downs of following Jesus today. When Jesus teaches His disciples, we should feel ourselves addressed by His words.

In this way, we see that the Gospels do not simply present us with facts to memorize but rather serve as tools by which God transforms us. As we watch the disciples and as we follow the life of Jesus Himself, we look into a mirror that reflects the quality of our own discipleship. And, of course, at the center of the Gospels stands Jesus, suffering and glorified.

20

ROOTED IN FAITH

Have you ever secretly wished you could steam open someone else's mail and read it? Here's an opportunity.

December 19

Dear Dan,

Great news! I can hardly believe it, but in any case, congratulations.

So now what are you going to do? Whatever you do, just be confident that the Lord is going to take care of you. He won't let you down. God has taken care of you before; don't you think He'll do so in this instance? And no matter what John says, you can do it. Don't let him get you down. You know he has weird ideas. He's dealing with his own anxieties.

Don't forget to get a present for Linda. The usual. But not too expensive. You know how she is, and I wouldn't want her to get angry.

Give the kids a kiss for me. And say hi to your mother. I've got to get going, but I hope to be able to get out there to visit you sometime soon. Maybe we can talk about why your church isn't growing any larger. I really don't think it's a problem with the size of the parking lot. I've been listening to the tapes of your sermons. They're practical enough, but where is the Gospel? The entire Old Testament looks forward to the coming of Christ—remember what Professor Clowney taught us in sermon class—so why aren't you bringing that out?

Oh well, a topic for another day. Talk soon.

Best,

Doug

Reading someone's personal correspondence is like eavesdropping on a private conversation. We're dropped into the middle of the dialogue with only a vague idea of what's really going on.

That is the way we approach much of the New Testament, which is composed of different letters. Though many were "circulars" meant to be read aloud to various churches, most of them were private letters. Yet they also target the heart of every believer; they are addressed to you and me as well as to the original audience.

READING THE APOSTLES' MAIL

The Gospels provide the bedrock of the New Testament, but the dominant literary form is the letter, or "epistle." As a matter of fact, twenty-one of the twenty-seven books of the New Testament are letters. Most of them flow from the pen of the energetic apostle Paul, who wrote to churches (in Galatia and Ephesus) and to individuals (Timothy, Titus, and Philemon). We also have letters from Peter, John, James, and Jude. One letter is anonymous—the book of Hebrews.

There are many differences between the letters. For instance, we've already noted that some of the letters speak to individuals, while others speak to entire churches. Further, some letters—such as the one to the Galatians—focus on local and individual problems while others, like Romans, Ephesians, and Hebrews read like general theological treatises.

Although all the letters do teach doctrine, we should not lose sight of the nature of these writings— *as letters.* God could have used the form of a theological or philosophical essay to communicate His truth to us. He could have chosen the debate form, or perhaps handed down sermons on ethical and theological topics. But He chose to correspond with us.

Why did God use the letter format? We may not be able to answer this question fully, but we can see how one special characteristic of a letter holds our interest: its personal quality. Letters are forms of intensely personal communication. They have an intimate, personal tone. As such, they convey the author's heart as well as his mind. For example, Paul's letters communicate his passion for the gospel and his love and concern for those to whom he wrote.

Whether the letter is addressed to a single group—one church or a group of churches as in the case of circular letters like Ephesians—or to an individual, it represents only one side of a conversation. Accordingly, letters emphasize the personal nature of Christian truth. Theology is not abstract; it is rooted in human experience. As Paul and the other apostles wrote about the nature of Christian truth, they packaged it in real-life situations.

Take, for instance, Paul's desire for unity in the church. Close fellowship among believers would send a powerful message to the outside world concerning the redeeming work of Christ—if Christians would only love one another and commit to living in peace! So Paul often taught about the unity of the church. But he didn't teach abstractly. He used real-life struggles. For example, he noted the conflict and "school spirit" that had infected the Corinthian church (see 1 Corinthians 1:10-17). People were following their favorite teachers and were drifting apart. Paul admonished them to follow the gospel of Jesus alone. In this way, he taught the importance of Christians standing together against a hostile world.

One consequence of the letter form is that occasionally we don't know the whole context. Take the letter that began this chapter. It leaves us with questions we can't answer with certainty. What was the "great news"? What was the usual present for Linda? What was so weird about John?

The New Testament letters leave us with similar questions. For instance, one of the most difficult questions facing interpreters of Paul's letters is: exactly who are his opponents? Frequently he wrote to a congregation to warn the church members about certain false teachers. Paul wrote to the Colossians, in part, to warn them of a dangerous philosophy that was affecting their fellowship (Colossians 2:6-23). The Colossians knew the exact nature of the danger, but we are left in the gray. We know certain traits the teachers exhibited but not the details of their false gospel message. We know that the heretics displayed qualities found later among the so-called Gnostics. They also shared characteristics with people who wanted to preserve elements of Judaism in Christianity. Yet, along with all we do know, we must allow for significant ambiguity as we attempt to interpret this letter and others.

THE SHAPE OF LETTERS

Letters have a certain form. We're familiar with the form of modern letters, like the one from Doug. And just like modern letters, New Testament letters follow certain ancient patterns in their form. For example, we find numerous similarities between New Testament letters and ancient Greek letters. Both had a basic three-part structure — the salutation, the body of the letter, and the closing greetings and doxology. Let's use Romans as an example.

> Romans 1:1-7 is the *salutation*, which identifies the letter
> writer and greets the person to whom it is addressed.
> Romans 1:8–15:33 is the *body* of the letter.
> Romans 16 is the *closing greetings* and *doxology*.

The difference between biblical and secular letters comes through primarily in their content rather than in their style. But sometimes the radical content of a biblical letter altered the typical Greek style. For instance, a Greek letter would begin with the name of the sender followed by a list of the names of the recipients, followed by "Greetings" (which is the ancient equivalent to our "Dear"). However, Paul might expand this to talk about his own and the recipient's relationship with God and then offer a kind of prayer that would begin with the words "Grace and peace." Paul would often follow this up with a short thanksgiving to God. A good example comes through in the book of Philippians:

> Paul and Timothy, servants of Christ Jesus, to all the saints
> in Christ Jesus at Philippi, together with the overseers and
> deacons: Grace and peace to you from God our Father and
> the Lord Jesus Christ. (1:1-3)

The body of Paul's letters generally contained three distinct elements. Let's look at each one in more detail:

Autobiographical elements. The letters often give us information about Paul, particularly dwelling on how he related to the church. Paul shares his life with those who read his letters. After all, the letter substituted for his personal presence among them as their spiritual father and leader. Even if he couldn't be with them day after day, he could provide guidance from afar. Because of his role as an apostle and because of God's inspiration, these letters that were written for specific historical situations in the early church are also foundational for our faith and practice as followers of Jesus.

Didactic elements. Paul's letters, as well as the other New Testament letters, taught the churches what to believe and how to act. The Gospels intended to share the wonderful acts and teachings of Jesus. Written after Jesus lived, died, and rose from the dead, they told the story in a way that was relevant to the early church, addressing its particular needs. However, they did this subtly.

In contrast, the letters *explicitly* looked back to Jesus and gave the theological and ethical interpretations that formed the foundation of the Christian faith. This is why many Christians tend to concentrate on reading the epistles. No other part of the Bible speaks as directly to our theological concerns as the letters.

Apologetic elements. "Apologetics" is a technical term that refers to the defense of the Christian faith against the challenges of nonChristian philosophies and religions. That is, the letters defended a true understanding of the gospel, guarding the church against error. It's hard to see things in black and white, right and wrong, in our age of relativism. But Paul helps us recover that perspective. The letters often served this apologetic function.

In particular, because the enemies of Paul insisted that Christians have to do something to earn God's love, Paul was moved to strongly reemphasize the foundational teaching that one's relationship with God is not earned; it results from faith in Jesus Christ alone. Jesus rescues us and forgives our sin, not because of what we do, but because of His love and grace.

Paul's warnings should alert us to similar misunderstandings of the good news of Jesus Christ today. As good Protestant evangelicals, we may state quite clearly that we are saved by grace alone. Our actions and attitudes, however, may be similar to the heresy Paul spoke of. We may find ourselves, for instance, working hard for God. By doing so, we may subtly think we're earning credits with Him. We may then grow angry or disillusioned when God doesn't answer our prayers in the way we think He should: "How could God do this to me, after all I've sacrificed for Him!" Paul not only guards against ancient heresies but warns our hearts of the ways we subtly and not-so-subtly undermine the free offer of the gospel.

Of course, it's possible to misread Paul on this matter, and God used the other letter writers to protect us from going too far in the opposite direction. That is, they warn against presuming on the grace of God. For example, we understand James to be an attempt to counteract false representations of Paul's emphasis on God's grace by reminding his readers of what Paul also believed but did not emphasize—that is, faith without works is dead. If your faith doesn't produce a desire to live as Jesus wants you to, then that faith must be nonexistent.

James straightens out our modern thinking about the relationship between grace and works. He tells us that the practice of our faith—acting on what we believe—confirms our salvation by helping us work out what we know to be true. The more we practice our faith, the more our confidence in the gospel grows. We don't earn our salvation, but through our changed lives and obedience we act out the faith we have and prove that "the Way" is right and good.

The letters of the New Testament nurtured the faith of the early church. And they nurture us, who live at the turn of this millennium, in the kind of thinking and behavior that should characterize a disciple of Jesus Christ. They do this by having us look back at Christ's work during His earthly ministry and by inviting us to look forward to His coming again. In the meantime, they teach us how to live in the present, between the "yet, and not yet" of Jesus.

21

ILLUMINATING OUR PAST, PRESENT, AND FUTURE

With rapier wit, the cartoon caption made its point: "Fred is a self-made man, which shows what happens when you don't follow directions."

I had to chuckle, even while recognizing the wisdom here. Our natural tendency is to be completely self-centered as we attempt to "make" our lives. Why should we be concerned with how people react to what we do, as long as we can say at the end, "I did it my way"?

Paul, writer of biblical letters *par excellence,* clearly understood this penchant for pure self-sufficiency. He had once worked hard at constructing a religious career—his way—for many years.

But then he met Jesus.

Now he had heavenly directions to follow, and his first task was to take a long, hard look into the past.

LOOKING BACK TO JESUS

Paul looked back and saw Jesus, One who was the "very nature of God," who through humility and for the sake of others divested Himself of that glory to die on a cross. Paul called on himself and all Christians to look to Christ and exchange a selfish lifestyle for one characterized by a Christlike humility (See Philippians 2:1-11).

He represents the perspective of all the biblical letter writers. Though some of them knew Jesus well during His earthly ministry, they all wrote from the vantage point of looking back to Him, recalling His death and resurrection. And they pointed out the significance of Jesus' actions and teachings for the church, present and future.

But Paul didn't know Jesus during His earthly ministry. Paul appears for the first time in Acts, promoting violent opposition to the fledgling church. He was present at the murder of Stephen (8:1); and later, traveling to Damascus to continue his persecution of Christians, he was "still breathing out murderous threats against the Lord's disciples" (9:1). Then, just outside Damascus, the glory of the risen Christ literally knocks him flat. Like Augustine, Paul was changed to the core of his being when Christ revealed Himself, and he joyfully enslaved his zealous and powerful personality to serve Him and His church.

After his Damascus road experience, Paul saw the past in a new way. He saw Christ in a new way. According to his own confession, "from now on we regard no one from a worldly point of view. Though we once regarded Christ in this way, we do so no longer" (2 Corinthians 5:16). And, of course, he saw himself in a new way. He could no longer live the life of a "self-made man." From now on he would be Christ's man.

All of this had profound impact on what he would write to Christians—to us—in his letters. Specifically, what new insights characterized Paul's overall message? Consider these four:

1. He recognized that Christ was not dead and irrelevant. Obviously, meeting Jesus as Paul did would transform a person's point of view. Paul encountered Jesus alive, and he saw that this One he had long persecuted was no obstacle to true religion. Paul would preach the risen Christ as the centerpiece of true faith (See Romans 1:4; 1 Corinthians 9:1, 15:8). The Son of God was a living person Paul could know and love in a warm personal relationship.

2. He realized that Jesus was not only human but divine. Paul's experience of Christ went far beyond the bounds of any ordinary human relationship. Here was the incarnation of deity in human form. Jesus was, as later Christian theology would understand the writings of the New Testament letters, fully God (Romans 9:5, Philippians 2:11) and fully man (Romans 5:17-19, 8:3; Philippians 2:7). Christ is the very glory of God (2 Corinthians 4:6).

The New Testament letters also tell us that it is Jesus who provided our salvation. He stood in our place, so that we, sinful human beings, can have a relationship with Him. We can know Him and become like Him in His trust in God, His surrender to God's purpose, and His compassion for humanity.

3. He learned that we can do nothing to deserve God's love and salvation. Here is the exact opposite of the self-made philosophy, the creed by which Pharisee Paul had so diligently lived. Now he saw clearly: God gives us salvation freely and graciously.

The apostle spent a lot of time on this point because it was hard for his contemporaries to grasp, just as it's hard for us to understand and live by today. That is, our forgiveness is by grace, the free gift of God. We don't have to earn our acceptance; we receive it by surrendering ourselves to God. Then we can live in thankful obedience to Jesus who gave us this new life. We take new direction as we move from feeding self and its desires to seeking the glory of God. Human nature is such that we feel as though we have to work for our salvation. In response, the New Testament letters — especially Paul's — point us back to the cross of Christ.

4. He saw that everything, even good works, are the result of grace. Paul doesn't say that good works are unimportant or that effort on our part isn't required for Christian maturity. Perhaps nowhere is this better expressed for the contemporary disciple than in Philippians 2:12-13, where Paul tells Christians to "continue to work out your salvation with fear and trembling, for it is God who works in you to will and to act according to His good purpose." Paul encourages us to exert ourselves in the matters of our faith and to realize as we are doing it that God is working in us.

And this was Paul's burden. It was his job to share "the gospel of Christ" (Galatians 1:7) with people who would be lost without God working in them. This is the gospel he learned from Christ (See Galatians 1:11-23) and whose content is Christ. It was Paul's special mission to take this precious message of God's salvation in Jesus Christ beyond the bounds of Israel to the Gentiles (See Romans 15:16-18).

Yet Paul understood that the Christian life was more than a matter of looking back. If Jesus was raised from the dead, then He is alive today. And Christians are those who have a relationship with Jesus, which affects how they live in the present. Therefore, many of the letters of the New Testament spell out what it means to have a relationship with Christ in the here and now.

LIVING IN THE PRESENT

The New Testament letters speak clearly to us of our place in God's history of salvation. We find that we are in the same place as Paul, James, John, Peter, and those who first received their letters. We live between Christ's first and second coming, when the kingdom of God is here on earth but also yet to come in its entirety. How do the New Testament letter writers describe this time?

They tell us that the Christian life will not be marked with health, wealth, and worldly success. Rather, Christians will suffer the sufferings of Christ (See Philippians 1:29, 3:10; 2 Thessalonians 1:5; 2 Timothy 1:8; 1 Peter 2:18-21, 4:13). But it is not suffering for the sake of suffering. We *suffer* with Christ so that we might be *glorified* with Christ, for we follow His pattern of death and then resurrection (Romans 8:17). After all, according to Peter, Christ suffered for us (1 Peter 2:21, 3:18).

As we read the New Testament letters we can see that the trouble, disappointments, pain, loneliness, and suffering we all experience are not arbitrary and unexpected but rather the path to glory and ultimate union with God. As Paul said, "Our present sufferings are not worth comparing with the glory that will be revealed in us" (Romans 8:18). For this reason, we are told to endure suffering (Romans 12:12; 2 Timothy 2:3, 4:5; 1 Peter 2:19).

We hear of examples from around the world of believers who suffer in ways very similar to the ways Paul and the New Testament church suffered. From Israel we hear reports of Russian Jews, converted to Christianity, forbidden entry and citizenship in Israel. Palestinian Christians often find themselves the objects of suspicion among their Muslim neighbors.

Christians in the United States usually do not experience this type of blatant persecution, but we may suffer for the gospel in more subtle ways. My sixteen-year-old son, Timothy, attends a small private boy's school in the outskirts of Philadelphia where we live. A year and a half ago he became excited about the gospel and began sharing it with some of his friends. He found that FOCUS, an excellent ministry devoted to the students and faculty of such schools, provided wonderful support and leadership for him. After several months, other students have become interested in Christian commitment, and a small nucleus of believers has grown to about twenty-five students.

But recently a concerned student came to check out the Bible study. He feared the group was a cult and wouldn't touch the snacks offered to him. His family has now called the school administration to inquire about this "cult." So far the school has remained support-ive, but the pattern is all too familiar. Outsiders, unsympathetic to the gospel, cast aspersions on the motives and character of Christians. They think our belief in God is a "crutch" and that we're deceiving our-selves when we say there's more to life than what they value — money, prestige, and status. We become the objects of ridicule or anger.

Paul's response is, "What else should you expect?" We don't yet live in heaven. The world is fallen and hostile toward the Lord. Paul says that our faith doesn't deliver us from suffering, but it does give us hope that there's more to human existence than our present trouble.

LIVING OUT OF GRATITUDE

In our chapter on the Law, we saw that Paul in particular made it clear that no one earns a good relationship with God by being good. No one can be that good; left to our own devices, none of us are any good at all (Romans 3:9-20). Our relationship with God is totally due to Jesus — we owe Him everything.

We often forget that it's not just salvation we've received as a gift from God, but everything we have. Sometimes we fall into the trap of thinking that even though God has given us spiritual blessings, our hard work and natural-born talents account for the rest. We may begin to feel a lot of pride in ourselves.

Paul often reminds us that *everything* we have is a gift from the Father. If we're blessed with any money at all, it's a gift from God. If we have any talent at all, it's a gift. If we have any relationships that bring us joy, they're from the Lord. If we feel any sense of peace or confidence in our souls, that too comes from God. Whatever we have comes from the hand of God and should stir thankfulness within us.

I once heard the story of a man and woman who gave a sizeable contribution to their church to honor the memory of their son who was killed in the Viet Nam War. When the pastor announced the generous donation, a woman whispered to her husband, "Let's give the same amount for our boy!" Her husband said, "What are you talk-ing about? Our son wasn't killed." "That's just the point," she said. "Let's give it as an expression of our thankfulness to God for sparing his life!"

That's the attitude of gratitude! Yet all of us are the constant benefactors of God's incomparable grace throughout our lives. How, then, should we live?

It's not surprising that a good portion of the letters in the New Testament are devoted to ethical instruction—telling us the kind of behavior that pleases God and expresses our thanks to Him. These guidelines for Christian living often come in the form of imperatives. An imperative is a command—a direction for behavior. We need to keep an eye open for these imperatives as we read the New Testament epistles, remembering that God wants us to be open to all the commands, so we don't fall into the habit of pulling out certain ones while ignoring others. For instance, we may hear and obey Paul's commands to avoid drunkenness and lust (Romans 13:13) but read right over his warning to beware of anger (Colossians 3:8).

I like to think of the Christian life as a race, as Paul referred to it (Galatians 2:2, 5:7; 2 Timothy 4:7). In this light, God's commands are challenges to us, the "runners." We need to adopt a whole-body approach to working out, not just exercising one part of ourselves. God's commands point out to us the many areas where we still need spiritual growth.

Yet as we follow the ethical guidelines found in the epistles, we'll constantly keep in mind the proper relationship between grace and obedience. Our obedience does not produce God's grace; God's grace leads to our obedience. In Galatians 5:1 Paul stated, "It is for freedom that Christ has set us free." He follows this immediately with the guideline for living, "Stand firm, then, and do not let yourselves be burdened again by a yoke of slavery." The same pattern is found in Galatians 5:13 and 5:24 and can be found throughout the letters.

So the letters warn us to avoid two pitfalls—thinking we must obey certain regulations in order to have a relationship with God, and thinking that because we are saved by grace we can do whatever we want. Even Paul, the most outspoken proponent of God's grace, insisted that Christians must behave in a way that pleases God.

Paul knew that the goal of imitating God (Ephesians 5:1) is beyond us, so he gave us another example to follow—an example of a weak person finding his strength in God. That example was Paul himself. In 1 Corinthians 11:1 Paul put it plainly: "Follow my example, as I follow the example of Christ" (See also 1 Corinthians 4:16, Philippians 3:17, 1 Thessalonians 1:6). Paul did not want us to follow him in absolutely every aspect of his life. We can't do that any more than we can follow Christ in every aspect of His life. We are not apostles, and we certainly aren't divine. But we *are* made in the image of Christ, as was Paul, our elder brother, and we can follow the apostle as he suffered, struggled, and pursued the path to glory.

The point is, we not only learn from Paul the facts of the faith and the right road to obedience, we have a role model to follow. Paul's example should motivate us to look for other godly mentors — men and women who are more mature in the faith than we are, those who can encourage and challenge us to keep growing in Christ.

LOOKING AHEAD TO CHRIST'S RETURN

Paul not only looked to the past as the source of our salvation, he looked to the future. Paul and all the letter writers, to a certain degree, were aware that Jesus Christ would be coming again in the future to complete His work of salvation. Christ's death and resurrection assures the ultimate victory over Satan (Colossians 2:15), but the battle will continue (Ephesians 6:10-20) until Christ returns again to put a final end to all evil.

Paul spoke frequently of Christ's return. He often referred to the future appearance of Jesus as "the Day of Christ" (1 Corinthians 5:5, 2 Corinthians 1:14, Philippians 1:10). From Paul we learn that this will be the day of final judgment against all God's enemies. Those who place their faith in Christ, suffering with Him in the present, will be saved from their oppression. A glorious day is coming. Indeed, the future casts its shadow back on the present in a sense because Paul wanted us to live as if Christ were coming back at any moment (1 Corinthians 7:29).

Paul was an apocalyptic thinker — a man who knew that the end of the world was a certain reality. Therefore, we should live — and Paul challenged us to live — with the expectation that Christ may return at any moment. Paul wants us to know that though the present is chaos, though there is injustice and evil, God promises to set all things right in the future.

READING THE LETTERS FOR SPIRITUAL GROWTH

In this short chapter, we haven't even begun to unearth all the riches of the epistles' treasures. I encourage you to dig in for yourself! As you do, keep these guidelines in mind:

1. Remember, the epistles are letters. You may not be able to understand everything to which the letter writers allude. They are talking to specific people, so they're tailoring their comments to specific problems. Be careful not to make absolute statements based on a letter that intends to speak to a specific situation.

2. Get a feel for the structure of each book you read. First, see where the greeting ends and the body of the letter begins. Note the way the author concludes the letter. Then look at the change of topics within the body of the letter. The writers deal with a host of issues and problems within a single epistle, but there is usually a topical arrangement.

3. Note what the letter writer says about himself. What can you learn from Paul or the other letter writers that builds your faith and helps you to please God? How should you appropriately imitate Paul and the other apostles?

4. Observe how the letter writers defended the faith against the challenges of their day. Many false teachers tried to dilute the gospel in the early days of Christianity, and the pattern continues today. What can you learn about defending the faith against attacks in our day?

5. Ask yourself, "What does the epistle teach me about God and my relationship with God?" Then look for the practical guidance offered. The indicative of Christian theology leads to the imperative of Christian ethics. How are you to behave in the light of what Jesus Christ has done for you?

The letter writers of the Bible constantly looked into the future. Indeed, the future coming of Christ was their blessed hope. We, too, look for a new heaven and a new earth in which righteousness dwells. As we turn now to the last of the major types of biblical literature — apocalyptic — we'll have an opportunity to explore this type of thinking even further.

22

IMAGES OF
THE END

It was midnight, and Susan couldn't sleep. For months she'd been waiting for this day, and now it had passed. Nothing had happened, absolutely nothing.

Susan started to cry. She felt empty in the pit of her stomach as she contemplated the days ahead. Most likely she would experience some ridicule, but she mostly feared the pity.

How great it would have been, though! All of her problems would have been washed away and she would now be experiencing the bliss of eternity. Instead, she had to get out of bed in the morning and face her husband and then her coworkers—not to speak of her bills. She had run up her credit card balance way beyond its limit so she could support a pamphlet ministry warning the unsaved of impending Judgment Day. Her husband didn't understand her and they'd had a number of fights about it, but she didn't see a need to be fiscally responsible when there was no reason to worry about October's payment. After all, if Jesus was coming in September. . . .

But it was now October 1. What went wrong? It wasn't as if she'd accepted her pastor's interpretations of the Bible hook, line, and sinker. She'd done the word studies, the mathematical computations, and the other important exegetical steps she'd learned in the church's Sunday school class. They checked out. She had also avoided reading the tainted interpretations of other commentators and scholars—people her pastor had warned would lead them astray.

And Pastor Lamp couldn't be wrong. He had shown them very carefully that the genealogies of Genesis proved creation took place in 11,006 B.C. He had proved to them the special importance of the number 13 in the Bible. If 12 was the number of completion, then 13 was the number of super-completion. Obviously, God intended the world to last for 13,000 years. How amazing that there were really thirteen, not twelve tribes of Israel—counting Joseph (one of the twelve sons of Jacob) twice since his sons Ephraim and Manasseh were the ones who received tribal allotments. And there were really thirteen, not twelve, apostles—counting Judas, and Matthias who replaced him.

Countless other hidden prophecies pointed to this prophetic reality. It had been awe-inspiring to see how Pastor Lamp made the difficult images of Daniel and Revelation so clear. And she'd had no doubt as he applied it all to modern events.

But that was yesterday.

Now she tried to force down the gnawing doubt. She got up from her bed and opened her Bible to read, once again. . . .

> The man clothed in linen, who was above the waters of the
> river, lifted his right hand and his left hand toward heaven,
> and I heard him swear by him who lives forever, saying, "It
> will be for a time, times and half a time. When the power
> of the holy people has been finally broken, all these things
> will be completed." (Daniel 12:7)

A COMMON STORY

Susan's struggles with prophecy may strike you as pure fantasy. After all, though there have been people who read the apocalyptic writings in the Bible and come away confused, having little desire to spend much more time trying to digest them, things were different in this case. Here, the fiction comes close to reality. Since World War II there have been more than two hundred predictions of the Second Coming based on apocalyptic literature.[1] The story above is a somewhat fictionalized version of one such prediction that took place in the mid-1990s.

Apocalyptic literature is perhaps the most difficult biblical genre for contemporary Christians to interpret. In large part this is due to the strange imagery that prevails. Hybrid beasts arise out of a chaotic sea to fight a human figure riding a cloud chariot (Daniel 7). A seven-headed sea beast also emerges from the ocean to fight an imposing figure riding a white horse and having a sword coming out of his mouth (Revelation 13, 19:11-20). Seals are broken, bringing worldwide calamity (Revelation 6-8); a prostitute rides a scarlet beast (Revelation 17); a new Jerusalem appears out of nowhere (Revelation 21). What does it all mean?

And then there are the numbers. They seem so precise, yet they are also shrouded in mystery. Daniel 9:25-27 is typical:

> Know and understand this: From the issuing of the decree
> to restore and rebuild Jerusalem until the Anointed One,
> the ruler, comes, there will be seven 'sevens,' and sixty-two
> 'sevens,' the Anointed One will be cut off and will have
> nothing. The people of the ruler who will come will
> destroy the city and the sanctuary. The end will come as a
> flood: War will continue until the end, and desolations
> have been decreed. He will confirm a covenant with many
> for one 'seven.' In the middle of the 'seven' he will put an
> end to sacrifice and offering. And on a wing of the temple
> he will set up an abomination that causes desolation, until
> the end that is decreed is poured out on him.

Are these the materials God has given us to construct a prophetic calendar of the end? If not, then what are they? Before addressing these questions directly, we need to see that apocalyptic literature is closely related to prophecy because it, too, looks at the present in the light of the future. There are enough differences with classical prophecy, however, that apocalyptic writing deserves a special mention in our survey of biblical genres.

WHAT IS APOCALYPTIC LITERATURE?

The term *apocalypse* comes from a Greek word meaning "to uncover, or lift up, what has been hidden under." It is most simply translated "revelation." It is the first word in the Greek text of the book of Revelation, explaining this book's English appellation (and why it is occasionally called the Apocalypse of John).

Some books and parts of books in the Old Testament are very similar to Revelation and are also called apocalyptic: Daniel (particularly chapters 7-12), Zechariah, Joel, and Isaiah 24-27, are examples of apocalyptic writing in the Old Testament. Most such examples come from late in the history of Israel, and there are many examples of noncanonical apocalypses written in the period of time between the testaments. The book of Enoch is perhaps the best known and is actually included in some contemporary Bibles whose traditions recognize certain apocryphal books.

The term *apocalypse* has entered our everyday language. It's not uncommon to hear our time in history described as an "apocalyptic age." In terms of everyday usage, the word indicates the end of history—and even further, the violent end of history.

This usage isn't too far from the biblical reality. The books listed above as apocalyptic, each at least in part, describe the process and end of history in violent terms. Daniel 7 pictures evil empires as hybrid beasts against which the Son of Man and the saints of the Most High do battle. The book of Zechariah closes with a description of the Day of the Lord when God will lead His holy army to destroy His enemies and save His people. Jesus Christ appears on a white horse leading an army against the forces of evil in Revelation 19. Thus, apocalyptic literature contains prophecy in the distant sense, with vivid images of the end of time.

PICTURES OF THE END

Like prophecy, of which it is a type, apocalyptic literature often begins in the present and then turns to the future. The main difference between prophecy and apocalypse has to do with the scope of its vision. While apocalyptic writing does refer to the near future, it goes far beyond the next few years—or even the next few centuries—to anticipate the end of history as we know it. Daniel 7 is a concise example. Let's look into it for more insight about apocalyptic writings.

In this chapter Daniel records a vision he experienced while he was lying in bed. He sees the coast of the sea, the waves dashing against the beach. Out of the sea emerges the first of four beasts—a hybrid. At first it appears as a lion with eagle's wings, but then it transforms into a human being. After the first, a second beast appears—a bear. The emphasis is on its two-sided nature as it lifts itself up and chews on three ribs. The third beast is a monster with mixed characteristics. Apparently its body is that of a leopard, but it also has four wings and four heads.

Little detail accompanies the description of the fourth and last monster to emerge from the sea. Indeed, no known animal is mentioned, the focus being on the iron teeth that devour those who stand before it, and its ten horns. The vision of this terrifying beast continues as a new horn appears, uprooting the first three and self-confidently boasting.

The scene then dramatically shifts to another realm. Here we discover rather humanlike figures. First an old man, called the Ancient of Days, seated on His throne. The scene is awe-inspiring, conveying a flame-engulfed throne, a river of fire flowing out from it, and countless thousands of people in a courtroom. Into His presence comes a second human-like figure, riding the clouds. He "was given authority, glory and sovereign power; all peoples, nations and men of every language worshiped him. His dominion is an everlasting dominion that will not pass away, and his kingdom is one that will never be destroyed" (Daniel 7:14).

The picture is just incredible. We gain a sense of power in both parts of the chapter, evoking feelings of horror and awe. But what are we to make of it all? It seems too strange, too weird for us to grasp. And we aren't the only ones to have this reaction: "I, Daniel, was troubled in spirit, and the visions that passed through my mind disturbed me. I approached one of those standing there and asked him the true meaning of all this" (Daniel 7:15-16).

Almost always in apocalyptic writing a supernatural being assists with the interpretation. God uses His angelic creatures to guide the person who receives the revelation toward the meaning of the vision or dream, though the one who receives the message is always left—as we often are—with a great measure of mystery. In this case, the angelic interpreter gets right to the heart of the first half of the vision: "The four great beasts are four kingdoms that will rise from the earth." Interestingly, the angel does not then go on and give clear and decisive identification of the four kingdoms or of the subsequent horns. It's enough to say that world history will be characterized by successive human governments that will be sources of fear and danger to God's people.

We can make some probable identifications, of course, but the further we go in the list the more difficult that becomes. It's important to note that the vision begins in Daniel's time. That is, the first beast is most likely Babylonia, the empire in power at the time Daniel receives the vision.[2] Though apocalyptic writing is ultimately concerned about the end of history, it begins, like prophecy, in the present.

While the first beast roots the prophecy in Daniel's day, the following beasts stretch out the vision into the indefinite future. The repeated description of future kingdoms as hybrid beasts magnifies the evil of these human kingdoms. The fact that the beasts are made up of more than one type of animal would have produced a reaction of horror and revulsion in the original Israelite readers. The Old Testament creation account makes it clear that God's original creation kept every one of God's creatures separate; they were created "according to their kind." The laws in Deuteronomy go to great pains to prohibit any mixing of different animals or even material fabric (22:9-11).

Even the setting of the vision has symbolic overtones and adds to the horror of the scene. By the time Daniel lived and wrote, in the sixth century B.C., the sea was a well-established image for denoting the forces that stood against God. God was the one who established order out of chaos and the sea represented a reversion to chaos. At times in poetic literature, God was the One who waged war against the sea (Psalm 77, 114; Nahum 1) and its monsters (Leviathan, Psalm 74).[3]

Further study shows that much of the imagery of this chapter — the sea image, for example — comes from the ancient Near East. From before the time the Bible was written, the religious literature of people like the Canaanites and the people of ancient Mesopotamia saw the creator-gods as locked in combat with the forces of chaos represented by a sea deity. The Bible, especially in poetic and apocalyptic passages, utilized imagery from the broader cultural background of the Israelites.

A similar phenomenon occurs in the second half of the vision. The cloud rider is also a well-established biblical image by the time of Daniel's vision. God rode the clouds into battle, according to passages like Psalm 18:11-12, 68:4, 104:3; Jeremiah 4:13; and Nahum 1:3. The clouds are the battle chariot of God, which makes it obvious that the "one like the son of man" is a divine figure. This picture image, like that of the sea, has an ancient Near Eastern background. In ancient Canaanite documents the god Baal is frequently called "the cloud rider." Once again God uses images that are well known in the surrounding culture in order to communicate truth about Himself.

The principle we need to recognize in our reading of biblical apocalypse is that at least a good part of the material that strikes us as strange was not strange to the original audience. They knew the images well from earlier Scripture and from their broader cultural background. Since we are no longer in direct contact with these traditions we must do some study and research to recover a better understanding of these passages. Even without this kind of research and study we can still understand the basic message of apocalyptic writing and Daniel 7 in particular. But if we take advantage of all the resources available to us, our understanding will be far richer and possibly more accurate.

The climax of Daniel 7 comes when the two realms, the evil human kingdoms represented by hybrid beasts and the divine realm represented by human images, clash. Initially, the evil human kingdoms will appear to dominate the world, destroying everything before them. But here is what happens with a simple decision from the Ancient of Days:

> Power will be taken away and completely destroyed forever. Then the sovereignty, power and greatness of the kingdoms under the whole heaven will be handed over to the saints, the people of the Most High. His kingdom will be an everlasting kingdom, and all rulers will worship and obey him. (Daniel 7:26-27)

VICTORY ASSURED

Apocalyptic writing rips away the veil that separates us from heaven. God calls the prophet and shows him what is in store for the future. By narrating his vision, the prophet gives us a highly symbolic picture of what is to come.

God both reveals and conceals as He speaks to us in the apocalyptic poetic images. He informs us accurately but not with precision. We get the basic point but not necessarily all the details. I came across a little story that perfectly illustrates what I'm saying:

> There was no gymnasium on our seminary campus, so we played basketball in a nearby public school. The janitor, an old black man with white hair, would wait patiently until the seminarians had finished playing. Invariably he sat there reading his Bible.
>
> One day I went up to him and inquired, "What are you reading?"
>
> The man did not simply reply, "The Bible." Instead he answered, "The book of Revelation."
>
> With a bit of surprise, I asked, "The book of Revelation? Do you understand it?"

"Oh yes," the man assured me. "I understand it."

"You understand the book of Revelation! What does it mean?"

Very quietly that old janitor answered, "It means that Jesus is gonna win."[4]

Yes, Christ's victory is the overall theme of Daniel, Revelation, and all the Bible's apocalyptic literature. But we might still wonder: Is it wrong to press God's message in these books for literal details of the end? Even though countless others have tried and failed, is it wrong to try? If that's not what apocalyptic writing is for, what is its purpose?

23

APOCALYPSE: OUR FUTURE HOPE

Shaphat ben Adlai walked by the gymnasium with disgust. He saw the well-tanned bodies and oiled hair of the Greeks as they left the building with smiles on their faces. A gymnasium in Jerusalem! The thought disgusted Shaphat, but that situation paled in comparison to what they were doing to the temple. Greek idols in the temple of the Lord! Oh God, how long?

He could take the constant abuse. He was ready even for death, if that should come. But he worried about his sons and daughters.

He quickly entered the secret gathering of fifteen men. The rabbi had already opened the scroll and was reading from the *Ketubim* (the Writings) a passage from the prophet Daniel. That prophet had lived hundreds of years ago, yet everything he described seemed so similar to Shaphat's own time. In the prophecy, it wasn't the

Greeks who controlled Jerusalem and the people of God; it was the Babylonians, and then the Persians. *God's people have been under the oppression of the wicked for so long!* he thought.

Shaphat knew the words well, but they worked their wonders upon him. *Yes, we are living in the time of conflict. The time when the beasts, the wicked and contemptible kingdoms of the world, control our material lives.*

But Shaphat knew this was not the end of the story.

God will break in some day! Perhaps it will be tomorrow. Perhaps a century or two from now. Perhaps even longer. Who knows?

Shaphat knew without a shadow of a doubt that present realities were not ultimate realities. God would reverse the situation, and those who sought Him would no longer be the fodder of the wicked.

WHY APOCALYPTIC STYLE?

Today many people use a form of apocalyptic writing as a kind of calendar of the end times. Ears prick up when someone claims to have discovered the key to unlocking the mysteries of future events. Yet the purposes of apocalyptic writing in the Bible go beyond satisfying our chronological curiosity. Shaphat knew it, and we should know it, too — that these writings offer great comfort and hope.

Present comfort. Jesus Christ is at the center of apocalyptic writing, both in the Old and New Testaments. New Testament passages (such as Matthew 24:30, Mark 13:26, Luke 21:27 and Revelation 1:7) identify the cloud rider in Daniel 7:13 (the one "like a son of man") with Jesus Christ. Apocalyptic writing's ultimate message is that Christ is coming again as a warrior to rescue His people from this present evil world. In the process He is going to destroy all earthly and heavenly evil. The point is: all of this is to comfort us as we struggle with present circumstances. God has completed the script of history, and it will turn out exactly as He has written it.

Some apocalyptic passages can give the impression, if wrongly read, that we can know all the details of that script today — especially when Christ is coming again. Or more generally, some people claim that apocalyptic passages give us signs to look for when the time is near. Jesus did tell the disciples before His death to be on the lookout for the "signs of the time," which are the appearance of false messiahs, wars, earthquakes, and famines (see Matthew 24, Mark 13, Luke 21). So at the turn of the Millennium, what do we see all around us? Many wars, a number of earthquakes, reports of famines, and even the appearance of false messiahs. Clearly we must be near the end!

But Jesus' words, delivered in the same speech, ought to continue echoing in the back of our minds:

> "No one knows about that day or hour, not even the angels in heaven, nor the Son, but only the Father. Be on guard! Be alert! You do not know when that time will come. It's like a man going away: He leaves his house and puts his servants in charge, each with his assigned task, and tells the one at the door to keep watch.
>
> Therefore keep watch because you do not know when the owner of the house will come back—whether in the evening, or at midnight, or when the rooster crows, or at dawn. If He comes suddenly, do not let him find you sleeping. What I say to you, I say to everyone: 'Watch!'" (Mark 13:32-37)

Jesus seems to give us a road map to the end and then tells us we can't use it to find the end of the road. Is this a contradiction?

Of course not. Jesus' purpose in the whole thirteenth chapter of Mark is to tell the disciples—and tell us through them—one thing: we must always be ready for His return.

The signs of the time listed here and elsewhere in the New Testament are always present. There have been wars, famines, earthquakes, and false messiahs from the time of Christ's death and resurrection to the present day. These things continually remind us that we're living in the time before Christ's coming. When we hear a report of another war, we're not to say, "Maybe this is the sign of the end!" Rather, we're reminded that we're still living in the time period between the first and second comings of Christ—the time when the world still suffers under the curse of the Fall.[1]

If it isn't the purpose of apocalyptic writings to give us a secret knowledge of the time of Christ's return, what good is it? And how does apocalyptic writing function as a mirror and a seed, as we have said all Scripture does?

Apocalyptic literature speaks to all believers who find themselves struggling in an evil world, no matter the time or place. Shaphat ben Adlai, in our fictional account, understood this. The setting was a real one: Jerusalem under the oppression of the Greek Seleucid kingdom in the middle of the second century B.C. He lived at a time when idol worshipers controlled the politics and attempted to force the people of God into shameful religious and cultural practices.

The Bible tells us that all of us live under the thrall of worldly evil. God's people in Iran today greet the message of apocalyptic writing with more urgency than those of us in the democratic West—but it's a matter of *degree* and not a difference in *kind*.

The purpose of apocalyptic writing is to provide comfort to the people of God in the midst of struggle, pain, and trouble. Not only is it a misuse to try to discover the date of the end or any other secret knowledge, it's a mockery of the gospel. After hundreds and even thousands of such perverse interpretations through the centuries, we might think we'd learn. But charlatans and worse will continue to use these wonderfully powerful passages of Scripture to tear down the church rather than build it up. Careful students of the Bible need to be especially wary, as we approach the new millenium, to avoid supporting what will surely be an increase in the abuse of these passages of Scripture.

Future hope. We do need present comfort, but we also need hope for the future. Life is hard. Even as Christians we still struggle. We experience the heartache of disappointment, sickness, death, and failed relationships. We continue to sin and to be the object of sin. If the present is all there is, it wouldn't be worth the effort, would it?

I think of a line from Isaac Singer's play, *The Cafeteria:* "We sit; we eat rice pudding. In between raisins we wonder who's next?" A man makes that statement, an elderly holocaust survivor, as he sits with his cronies in a New York eatery. They are always there, talking and ordering rice pudding, debating the meaning of life, telling jokes, sharing sad stories. The man reminds us that we do constantly face a daunting truth of our existence: the fact of death. The play is about love and how we can find it, but love is not the only word spoken into our lives, not the only calling asking for (and, in the case of death, *demanding*) a response. We can accept or refuse the invitation to love, but we cannot ignore the summons of death.

But God reveals to us in apocalyptic passages that death is not the final scene. Death is followed by resurrection. Seeming defeat gives way to victory. Wrongs will be righted and evil will be defeated once and for all.

Christianity has been criticized as a religion that focuses too much on the future, avoiding the problems of the present. We've been accused of longing for that "pie in the sky by and by." Certainly there are emphases within Christianity that deserve this kind of parody. We should never avoid the problems nor denigrate the pleasures of the present by simply ignoring all things but future heavenly realities. We need to work to better ourselves, our churches, and our society.

However, we can do this work while still recognizing that things will never be made perfect this side of heaven. We may stave off the forces of danger and decay, but they will never disappear. Our ultimate hope, according to biblical apocalypse, is our continued relationship with God after death in heaven.

The hope God wants to create within us is not a mere wishful desire for something that may or may not come. Biblical hope is the confidence that God will not let present realities continue. Evil may appear to be on top right now, and it may always have the upper hand in this world. But it is absolutely certain, beyond any doubt, that God will right all wrongs in the future. God wants us to stay rooted in the present, but He engenders a future hope in us. He does this through the powerful images we find in apocalyptic literature, especially those images in the last two chapters of Revelation.

These chapters bring to culmination a number of themes initiated in the Old Testament. First, God the warrior wins the ultimate victory over the forces of evil. Revelation 19:11-20 pictures Jesus Christ, armed with a sword, leading the heavenly army in the final battle against the beast and His armies. This climaxes the battle between the kingdom of God and the kingdom of Satan that began as early as Genesis 3, when the fall into sin created a conflict between those who followed God and those who continued in the way of the serpent.

It is also in the last chapters of Revelation that we hear of the coming of the New Jerusalem. Jerusalem was the place where God chose to meet His people with special intimacy during the Old Testament period. God made His presence known there, and those who wanted to meet with Him would journey to that city. The New Jerusalem, unlike its Old Testament precursor, is a description of the whole of the new heavens and new earth. That is, *everywhere* is now Jerusalem, the place where God dwells. As a matter of fact, there's no need for a temple in the New Jerusalem (21:22) because God's presence permeates all of the city.

This city has a river, and on both banks of this river is a garden. The garden has not just one, but many trees of life. Eden is restored, yet it's something better than original Eden! Revelation 22, the last chapter of the Bible, thus brings us back to the first two chapters of Genesis. Thanks to the work of Christ, God's people find themselves completely restored in their relationship with God, enjoying the bliss of being in His presence.

READING APOCALYPTIC LITERATURE
FOR SPIRITUAL GROWTH

The apocalyptic style is not an esoteric code language that provides the grist for our speculations about the future. The apocalyptic teaching of the Bible gives us a vision of the future that generates hope in the present. We must not avoid reading it because it's difficult to understand or because it may be unsettling. As you read apocalyptic passages, consider the following guidelines.

1. Review the principles involved in reading prophecy and poetry. Apocalyptic writing is a special kind of prophecy, so the principles involved there are helpful here. Some apocalyptic writing is presented in a poetic format, so you'll benefit from knowing how to interpret poetry.

2. Be reserved. Apocalyptic writing, like prophecy, uses a lot of imagery (see Numbers 12:6-8). Imagery communicates its message truly and accurately but not precisely. The use of numbers (such as 7, 10, 1,000, and others) gives the impression of precision, but they, too, are usually symbolic. Be careful not to press the language of the apocalyptic seers into an unwarranted literalism.

3. Bring out your commentaries. Much of the apocalyptic imagery has an ancient historical background that a good commentary or reference book can illuminate.

4. Ask questions. How is Christ presented in this passage? How does this passage relate to my present circumstance? In what ways does it comfort me in the present?

Apocalyptic writing invites us to live for the future. We don't lose touch with the present, but we're always mindful of what is coming. Christ's kingdom is with us now in seed form, but its full manifestation is coming at the end of the age. We don't know when that will be, but we must be ready.

In the meantime, God inspires us to keep taking on the character of Christ as He gives us the picture of the new kingdom, which is our eternal inheritance. In response to this great vision, at the conclusion of the Bible we say with John, "Amen. Come, Lord Jesus."

THE LAST WORD

We began our journey of reading the Bible with heart and mind with a reference to the parable of the sower, in which the Word is likened to a seed (Matthew 13:1-23). The seed has the potential for growth if planted in good soil. Otherwise, it will die.

As we, receptive readers eager for God's transformation, encounter His Word, we too will grow. As we appropriate the Word into our lives, we will find ourselves becoming more and more like its author, the triune God.

A seed doesn't yield all of its growth in a microsecond, however. Growth is a process. Likewise, reading the Bible doesn't produce a magical transformation of heart and mind. We must read the Word carefully and thoughtfully. We'll struggle with passages and books that are hard to understand. And we'll fight against the tendency to reject passages we understand all too clearly but don't want to believe or obey. As we read the Word to let it take root within us, we need to read in such a way that we invite it to transform our lives.

We also read the Word like a mirror of our soul. Through our encounter with God's Word, we have a clearer sense of who we are—on the inside. Of course, God uses this as well to cause us to change in a way that makes us more like Him.

We also noted early in the book, that the Bible's focus is on Jesus Christ, fully God and fully human, who died on the cross for our sins and was raised in glory. Whether we read the Old or the New Testament, we are constantly confronted with the Good News.

As you continue to read the most important Book of all time, I hope you'll keep the following questions in mind:

1. What does this passage of the Bible teach me about God and my relationship with Him? The answer to this question should arouse a sense of awe and love that expresses itself in worship.

2. What does this passage tell me about how God has acted in the past? The answer to this question shows God's love for His people. It should encourage our faith and kindle hope as we face problems in the present.

3. How does this passage change the way I think about the world and how does it impact the way I live my life? The answer to this question allows me to worship God with my whole being as I obey Him out of gratitude for what He has done.

4. How has God chosen to communicate these truths to me through the Scriptures? Think of the different genres God uses to capture our imaginations and transform our lives.

5. How does this passage present Christ? How does it anticipate His suffering and His glorification? How do I respond to this good news?

The Word of God is rich, complex, challenging, and compelling. As long as we live, we will struggle to understand it. But as long as we struggle with it, we will grow. I have attempted to encourage a lifetime adventure of Bible study and spiritual growth. The Bible's cornucopia of literary genres invites continued reflection. To read the Bible with heart and mind consistently is to enter into a lifelong conversation with God. And this conversation has only one possible result: continued growth and transformation into the image of Jesus Christ.

NOTES

PREFACE

1. John Bunyan, *Grace Abounding to the Chief of Sinners*, as quoted in Frank Mead, ed., *12,000 Religious Quotations* (Grand Rapids: Baker, 1989).
2. Prayer from Singapore, the Church Missionary Society, in Roberts, Elizabeth and Elias Amidon, *Earth Prayers from Around the World* (San Francisco: HarperSanFrancisco, 1991), p. 304.
3. John Calvin, *The Institutes*, as quoted in E. Paul Hovey, *The Treasury of Inspirational Anecdotes* (Grand Rapids: Revell, 1994).

CHAPTER 1. THE WORD IS THE SEED

1. The following block quotes from Augustine are found in his *Confessions*, excerpted in Richard Foster and James Bryan Smith, eds., *Devotional Classics* (San Fransisco: HarperSanFrancisco, 1993), pp. 52-55.
2. Augustine, quoted in Frank Mead, ed. *12,000 Religious Quotations* (Grand Rapids: Baker Book House, 1989), p. 50.
3. Paul Little, *How to Give Away Your Faith*, quoted in Jim Townsend, *Old Testament Highlights* (Elgin, IL: David C. Cook, 1987), p. 51.
4. Karl Barth, as described in Frederick Buechner, *Wishful Thinking* (San Francisco: HarperCollins, 1993), pp. 10-11.
5. Augustine, quoted in *12,000 Religious Quotations*.

CHAPTER 2. THE MIRROR OF OUR SOULS

1. See Tremper Longman III, *How to Read the Psalms* (Downers Grove, IL: Inter-Varsity Press, 1988), p. 13.
2. Alan Jones, *Soul Making* (New York: Harper & Row), p. 166.
3. Sundar Singh, in Richard Foster's *Devotional Classics* (San Francisco: Harper-Collins, 1993), p. 310.
4. A. W. Tozer, *The Pursuit of God* (Alberta, Canada: Horizon House, 1976), p. 80.

CHAPTER 3. THE SURPRISING ENCOUNTER

1. At the time of Jesus' ministry, of course, what we call the Old Testament was the only Bible around. It was commonly referred to as "Moses," the author of the first five books, "and the Prophets," referring more generally to the authors of the rest of the books.
2. Gerald May, *The Awakened Heart* (San Francisco: HarperCollins, 1988), pp. 171-172.
3. Christina Bucher, *Biblical Imagery for God* (Elgin, IL: Brethren Press, 1995), p. 5.
4. John R. W. Stott, in James Hewett, *Illustrations Unlimited* (Wheaton, IL: Tyndale House, 1988), p. 44.

CHAPTER 4. A MATTER OF PERSPECTIVE

1. This topic is too broad to treat here. For a survey of the evidence please consult W. A. Grudem, "Scripture's Self-Attestation and the Problem of For-mulating a Doctrine of Scripture," in *Scripture and Truth*, D. A. Carson and J. D. Woodbridge, eds. (Grand Rapids: Zondervan, 1983), pp. 19-59.
2. Lady Jane Grey, in Van deWeyer, Robert, ed. *The HarperCollins Book of Prayers* (San Francisco: HarperSanFrancisco, 1993), p. 172.
3. Dag Hammarskjold, in *The HarperCollins Book of Prayers*, p. 186.

CHAPTER 5. A PASSIONATE APPROACH

1. I wish to acknowledge my indebtedness throughout this section to B. K. Waltke, "Hermeneutics and the Spiritual Life," *Crux* 23 (1987), pp. 5-11.
2. John Donne, lines from Sonnet XIV, quoted in *The Top 500 Poems* (New York: Columbia University Press, 1992), p. 88.
3. The metaphor and categories that follow come from Waltke, "Hermeneutics and the Spiritual Life," p. 11.
4. Henri Nouwen, *The Wounded Healer* (New York: Doubleday, 1972), p. 88.

CHAPTER 6. IS THE BIBLE TRUSTWORTHY?

1. There is a disagreement among evangelical scholars as to the time of the Exodus and Moses' leadership. Some believe the evidence points to a period of time in the thirteenth century B.C.
2. Serious students of the Bible should have introductions to the New and Old Testament in their libraries. These works give the dates and backgrounds to all the books of the Bible. Try R. B. Dillard and Tremper Longman III, *An Introduction to the Old Testament* (Grand Rapids: Zondervan, 1994) and D. A. Carson, D. Moo, and L. Morris, *An Introduction to the New Testament* (Grand Rapids: Zondervan, 1992).

3. See R. Beckwith, *The Old Testament Canon of the New Testament Church* (Society for the Promotion of Christian Knowledge, London, 1987).

4. If you want more detailed information about biblical textual criticism, ask your pastor for a good book dealing with the subject. It can be interesting, though heavy, reading. One excellent older book would be: J. Harold Greenlee, *Introduction to New Testament Textual Criticism* (Grand Rapids: Eerdmans, 1964).

5. Herbert Lockyer, *All the Doctrines of the Bible* (Grand Rapids: Zondervan, 1964), p. 8

CHAPTER 7. WHAT'S THE MEANING HERE?

1. Frederick Buechner, *Wishful Thinking* (San Francisco: HarperCollins, 1993), p. 9.

CHAPTER 8. HISTORY: READING IT AFRESH

1. I consider Moses, living in the fifteenth century B.C., to be this author, in spite of the arguments to the contrary. See R. B. Dillard and Tremper Longman III, *An Introduction to the Old Testament* (Grand Rapids: Zondervan, 1994), pp. 38-48.

2. See Tremper Longman III, "Nahum," in T. E. McComiskey, ed., *The Minor Prophets* (Grand Rapids: Baker, 1993), pp. 765-830.

3. For instance, see the important historical source presented by D. J. Wiseman Jr., *Chronicles of the Chaldaean Kings (626-556 B.C.)*, in the British Museum (London: British Museum, 1956).

4. See Tremper Longman, *Old Testament Commentary Survey*, 2nd. ed., (Grand Rapids: Baker, 1995). This book contains reviews of hundreds of commentaries that will give an introduction to archaeological surveys.

5. See "Daniel," in R. B. Dillard and Tremper Longman III, *An Introduction to the Old Testament* (Grand Rapids: Zondervan, 1994), pp. 329-352.

6. William Barclay, *The Daily Study Bible, Gospel of Luke* (Philadelphia: Westminster Press, 1975).

CHAPTER 9. HISTORY: LEARNING THE LESSONS OF THE PAST

1. The Valley of Achor was the place where Achan, the man who betrayed the Lord after the defeat of the city of Jericho, was defeated. In Hebrew the valley's name was "Trouble," but in this new exodus the entranceway into the land is given the name "Hope."

2. D. Hudson, "Come, Bring Your Story," Mars Hill 1 (1994), pp. 73-86.

CHAPTER 11. LAW: BEING FAITHFUL TO OUR DIVINE KING

1. The ancient Near Eastern treaties may be found in English translation in J. Pritchard, ed. *Ancient Near Eastern Texts*, 3rd ed. (Princeton, N.J.: Princeton University Press, 1969), pp. 201-206; 529-535.

2. Viktor Frankl, *The Will to Meaning* (New York: Meridian, 1988), p. 64.

CHAPTER 12. POETRY: TAKE A NEW LOOK

1. Ecclesiastes contains many prose statements as well.

2. F. Medicus, *Grundfragen der Asthetik* (Jena, Germany, 1907), p. 14, quoted in

Hans Urs von Balthasar, *The Glory of the Lord* (Edinburgh: T. & T. Clark, 1982), p. 43.

3. An interesting case has been made (G. Lakoff and M. Johnson, *Metaphors We Live By,* University of Chicago Press [Chicago, 1980]) that all language is metaphorical at root.

4. This is done in other handbooks, for instance, Tremper Longman III, *How to Read the Psalms* (Downer's Grove, IL: InterVarsity, 1988) and W. G. E. Watson, *Classical Hebrew Poetry: A Guide to Its Technique* (Journal of Old Testament Studies, 1984).

5. Eugene H. Peterson, *Living the Message* (San Francisco: HarperSanFrancisco, 1996).

CHAPTER 13. POETRY: LANGUAGE OF THE HEART

1. John Fischer, *True Believers Don't Ask Why* (Minneapolis: Bethany House, 1989).

2. A. E. Housman, *The Name and Nature of Poet,* as quoted in Justin Kaplan, ed., *Bartlett's Familiar Quotations,* 16th ed. (Boston: Little, Brown and Co., 1992).

CHAPTER 14. WISDOM: THE SUPREME GOAL

1. Daniel Goleman, *Emotional Intelligence* (New York: Bantam, 1995).

CHAPTER 15. WISDOM: FIND IT . . . *Where?*

1. See Job 28:12,20.

2. Oswald Chambers, *Shade of His Hand: Talks on the Book of Ecclesiastes* (Christian Literature Crusade).

3. Bernie S. Siegel, *Peace, Love, and Healing* (New York: Harper & Row, 1989), p. 191.

CHAPTER 16. THE PROPHETS: GOD'S COVENANT ENFORCERS

1. The dating of Joel is uncertain, but it is often placed this early. Isaiah and Micah contain prophecies that come from the time period after the destruction of the northern kingdom, as well as some that precede it. For details, consult the relevant chapters in R. B. Dillard and Tremper Longman III, *Introduction to the Old Testament* (Grand Rapids: Zondervan, 1994).

2. Jeremiah and Ezekiel, both being compendiums of long prophetic careers, contain prophecies that come from the time of the Exile as well as those that precede it.

3. Mary J. Evans, "Thus Says the Lord," in *The Bible User's Manual,* J. F. Balchin, D. H. Field, and Tremper Longman III, eds. (Leicester, England: InterVarsity/Scripture Union, 1991), p. 150.

4. Tremper Longman III, "Nahum," in *The Minor Prophets,* Thomas McComiskey, ed. (Grand Rapids: Baker, 1993), pp. 765-771.

5. Hal Lindsey, *The Late Great Planet Earth* (Grand Rapids: Zondervan, 1970), p. 166.

6. Gordon Fee and Douglas Stuart, *How to Read the Bible for All It's Worth,* 2nd ed. (Grand Rapids: Zondervan, 1993), p. 166.

CHAPTER 17. THE PROPHETS: HEARING THEM TODAY

1. C. S. Lewis, *God in the Dock* (Grand Rapids: Eerdmans, 1970), p. 58.
2. C. S. Lewis, *The Four Loves* (New York: Harcourt, Brace & Jovanovich, 1960), p. 13-14.
3. It's interesting to read Numbers 12:6-8 in the light of this question. The description of the prophetic message after the time of Moses as containing visions and riddles leads one to expect a high degree of figurative language.

CHAPTER 18. THE GOSPELS: MANUALS FOR DISCIPLESHIP

1. These are not to be confused with modern biographies. Ancient biographies are not so restricted in terms of a chronological presentation of the person's life. Also, ancient biographies are not as neutral as many modern ones. The Gospels were written to persuade people that Jesus is the Messiah. For an excellent summary of the gospel genre with bibliography, see L. W. Hurtado, "Gospel Genre," in *Dictionary of Jesus and the Gospels*, J. B. Green, S. McKnight, and I. H. Marshall, eds., (Downers Grove, IL: InterVarsity Press, 1992), pp. 276-282.
2. The first three books, commonly called the Synoptic Gospels, are the most alike. John shares many stories with them but does stand out.
3. This is especially true of those events surrounding the crucifixion of Christ— for example, Peter's denial (Matthew 26:69-75, Mark 14:66-72, Luke 22:54-62, John 18:15-18 and 25-27).
4. Jim Townsend, *Gospel Themes: Four Portraits of Christ's Life* (Elgin, IL: David C. Cook, 1987).
5. For the discussion of the historical relationship between the Gospels, see D. A. Carson, D. J. Moo, and L. Morris, *An Introduction to the New Testament* (Grand Rapids: Zondervan, 1992), pp. 19-60.
6. Iranaeus became Bishop of Gaul in A.D. 180 and wrote *Against Heresies* during 182–188 in an attempt to refute Gnostic doctrines.
7. Theophilus means "one who loves God," and so may refer to any Christian reader rather than to a specific individual. In any case, this introduction gives the gospel the feel of a personal dialogue.
8. See D. Bock, "Luke, Gospel of," in *The Dictionary of Jesus and the Gospels*, J. Green, S. McKnight, and I. H. Marshall, eds. (Downers Grove, IL: InterVarsity, 1992), p. 498, as well as his massive commentary on Luke, vol. 1 (Grand Rapids: Baker, 1995). Volume 2, by the same publisher, is forthcoming.
9. M. Travers, "Luke," in *A Complete Literary Guide to the Bible*, L. Ryken and Tremper Longman III, eds. (Grand Rapids: Zondervan, 1993), p. 401.
10. See M. Wilkins, "Discipleship," in *The Dictionary of Jesus and the Gospels*, J. B. Green, S. McKnight, and I. H. Marshall, eds., (Grand Rapids: Zondervan, 1992), pp. 182-189, as well as his books, *Following the Master: A Biblical Theology of Discipleship* and *The Concept of Disciple in Matthew's Gospel.*
11. Frederick Buechner, *The Magnificent Defeat* (San Francisco: Harper, 1985).

CHAPTER 19. THE GOSPELS: FOLLOWING OUR WARRIOR-TEACHER

1. For more on the three battle fronts, see Dan Allender and Tremper Longman III, *Bold Love* (Colorado Springs: NavPress, 1992).

CHAPTER 22. APOCALYPTIC LITERATURE: IMAGES OF THE END

1. See S. D. O'Leary, *Arguing the Apocalypse: A Theory of Millennial Rhetoric* (Oxford: Oxford University Press, 1994).
2. A number of considerations leads to this conclusion. For one thing, Babylonia's national symbols included both the lion and the eagle. Further, the transformation of the hybrid beast into a human reminds us of Nebuchadnezzar's own transformation in Daniel 4. Lastly, this fourfold kingdom scheme is similar to the one found in Daniel 2, and the first kingdom there is Babylon (2:38).
3. See Tremper Longman III and D. Reid, *God is a Warrior* (Grand Rapids: Zondervan, 1995), pp. 63-68.
4. Bernard Travaielle, in James S. Hewett, ed., *Illustrations Unlimited* (Wheaton, IL: Tyndale House, 1988).

CHAPTER 23. APOCALYPSE: OUR FUTURE HOPE

1. One of the best books on this subject is by Anthony Hoekema, *The Bible and the Future* (Grand Rapids: Eerdmans, 1979).

AUTHOR

TREMPER LONGMAN III is professor of Old Testament at Westmont College. For the past seventeen years, he had been professor of Old Testament at Westminster Theological Seminary in Philadelphia. Tremper has written a number of scholarly and popular books including *Bold Love, Cry of the Soul,* and *Intimate Allies* (with psychologist Dan Allender) and *An Introduction to the Old Testament* (with Ray Dillard) and *How to Read the Psalms* (IVP). In early 1998, Eerdmans published *Ecclesiastes* in the NICOT series. In the summer of 1998, he and Dan Allender published their fourth co-authored book entitled, *Bold Purpose* (Tyndale House). He was in charge of the poetical books for the production of the *New Living Translation.* Tremper is married to Alice and has three sons, Tremper (IV), Tim, and Andrew. In his spare time, he enjoys exercise and watching movies.